BIG STRUCTURES
LARGE PROCESSES
HUGE COMPARISONS

Also available in the
Russell Sage Foundation
75th Anniversary Series

Notes On Social Measurement
Historical and Critical
by Otis Dudley Duncan

BIG STRUCTURES
LARGE PROCESSES
HUGE COMPARISONS

Charles Tilly

RUSSELL SAGE FOUNDATION   NEW YORK

The Russell Sage Foundation

The Russell Sage Foundation, one of the oldest of America's general purpose foundations, was established in 1907 by Mrs. Margaret Olivia Sage for "the improvement of social and living conditions in the United States." The Foundation seeks to fulfill this mandate by fostering the development and dissemination of knowledge about the political, social, and economic problems of America. It conducts research in the social sciences and public policy, and publishes books and pamphlets that derive from this research.

The Foundation provides support for individual scholars and collaborates with other granting agencies and academic institutions in studies of social problems. It maintains a professional staff of social scientists who engage in their own research as well as advise on Foundation programs and projects. The Foundation also conducts a Visiting Scholar Program, under which established scholars working in areas of current interest to the Foundation join the staff for a year to consult and to continue their own research and writing. Finally, a Postdoctoral Fellowship Program enables promising young scholars to devote full time to their research while in residence for a year at the Foundation.

The Board of Trustees is responsible for oversight and the general policies of the Foundation, while the immediate administrative direction of the program and staff is vested in the President, assisted by the officers and staff. The President bears final responsibility for the decision to publish a manuscript as a Russell Sage Foundation book. In reaching a judgment on the competence, accuracy, and objectivity of each study, the President is advised by the staff and a panel of special readers.

The conclusions and interpretations in Russell Sage Foundation publications are those of the authors and not of the Foundation, its Trustees, or its staff. Publication by the Foundation, therefore, does not imply endorsement of the contents of the study. It does signify that the manuscript has been reviewed by competent scholars in the field and that the Foundation finds it worthy of public consideration.

Library of Congress Catalog Number: 84–60264
Standard Book Number: 0–87154–879–8

to SAMUEL HUNTINGTON BEER

*inspired teacher of Big Structures,
Large Processes, and Huge Comparisons*

FOREWORD

In 1982 the Russell Sage Foundation, one of America's oldest general purpose foundations, celebrated its seventy-fifth anniversary. To commemorate this long commitment to the support and dissemination of social science research, we departed from our customary publishing procedures to commission several special volumes. Unlike most Russell Sage books, which emerge as the end products of various Foundation-supported research programs, these Anniversary volumes were conceived from the start as a series of publications. In tone, they were to be distinctly more personal and reflective than many of our books, extended essays by respected scholars and authors on significant aspects of social research.

As befits an anniversary celebration, the volumes in this series address issues of traditional concern to the Foundation—social measurement techniques, research on women, the interaction of law and society. That choice of issues also reflects the Foundation's broader interest in analyzing and illuminating significant social changes. So it is appropriate that this volume, the second in our series, should focus specifically on strategies for the analysis of social change.

Charles Tilly approaches his subject from a distinctively historical perspective, asking how twentieth century social scientists have attempted to understand and explain the enormous social changes that marked the nineteenth and early twentieth centuries. He answers with a spirited indictment of many of the assumptions underlying standard social scientific theory and a persuasive argument for the importance of concrete and comparative historical research.

In its short and lucid span, *Big Structures, Large Processes, Huge Comparisons* encompasses a selective and imaginative literature review; a challenging agenda for future research; and some tantalizing glimpses of the author's own historical speculations. One of our hopes in commissioning these special Anniversary volumes was that they might appeal to scholars and interested general readers alike; we think this lively book demonstrates just how gracefully and well that hope can be realized.

MARSHALL ROBINSON
President
Russell Sage Foundation

PREFACE

Why do other people's books behave like docile marionettes? Mine keep playing Pinocchio. They take on characters of their own and resist correction. This one, for instance. When I sat down to write it, the book was supposed to end up mild-mannered, studious, and balanced: an even-handed survey of various ways to approach large comparisons of social structures and processes. Somehow it materialized as a bit of a bully. It struts around with a confident, pugnacious air. Yet behind the bravado hides a lazy, indecisive, pusillanimous weakling, with sticks for legs. My little book often makes accusations without naming names, avoids fights one might have expected it to welcome, and fails to specify when, where, or how alleged misdeeds occurred. Incorrigible!

Yet, for all its faults, I love the little rapscallion. The Russell Sage Foundation's invitation to write an essay on "comparative and interdisciplinary research in the social sciences" gave me a welcome chance to reflect on the strengths and weaknesses of the schemes we customarily use to analyze large social processes and to speculate on their origins. That part of the assignment kept me in familiar surroundings; I have spent many years studying large processes such as proletarianization, urbanization, and statemaking.

Given the drift of recent work on large processes, however, I felt I should also discuss the ways in which people analyze very large social structures such as systems of states and make comparisons among them. There I left my own turf: Although I have sometimes speculated on big structures and huge comparisons, and have read other people's work on the subject attentively, I have never undertaken serious empirical work of my own along those lines. When I have worked through huge comparisons for my own purposes, they have almost always fallen into the category this book calls "individualizing" comparisons: attempts to clarify the characteristics of the case at hand by means of contrast with another well-documented case. Familiarity with statemaking and collective action in France, for example, has often helped me think through the links between statemaking and collective action in Great Britain, and vice versa; but I have never undertaken a sustained comparison between the two states for the purpose of identifying principles of variation in statemaking, collective action, or the links between them. Thus I come to the discussion of large processes as an old hand, and to the discussion of big structures and huge comparisons as an interested outsider.

Nevertheless I enjoyed whittling the new log. Scattered thoughts and dissatisfactions, long accumulating, came together in a rush. Words tumbling onto the page. Some of them looked interesting enough to keep. The resulting book falls far short of documented intellectual history, systematic review of the literature, or close textual exposition and criticism. It comes closer to what the French call a *prise de position*: statement of a view to be argued and explored later on. An extensive bibliography of the work I have consulted on these matters will, I hope, provide some compensation for the book's failings. (Although almost all of the text is brand new, I did borrow much of chapter 4's discussion of Fernand Braudel from my "The Old New Social History and the New Old Social History," *Review* 7 (1984): 363–406.)

Many friends helped me chase down the nimble puppet. On very short notice, ample, thoughtful critiques of a first draft arrived from Rod Aya, Robert Cole, Frederick Cooper, Ronald Gillis, Raymond Grew, Michael Hechter, Lynn Hunt, Ira Katznelson, William Roy, James Rule, Theda Skocpol, Arthur Stinchcombe, Martin King Whyte, and Mayer Zald. They persuaded me to eliminate some defective ideas, to clarify some murky arguments, and to provide a bit more documentation for some of the book's less plausible notions. In a second round, Daniel Chirot, Robert Merton, and (again) Theda Skocpol offered various combinations of critique and encouragement. They caused another substantial series of revisions.

My critics did me the great compliment of taking the work seriously and stalking its errors relentlessly. Their critiques, regrettably, made it clear that no revisions I could make in the short run would convince any of them—much less all of them—that each of the book's arguments was correct. Absolve them and blame Pinocchio.

Charles Tilly
Ann Arbor
September 1984

CONTENTS

INTELLECTUAL EQUIPMENT

Worrying About Social Change

W e bear the nineteenth century like an incubus. Inspect the map
of almost any American city. Notice the telltale marks: rail lines slic-
ing one section from another; a speculator's grid, with its numbered
rectilinear streets and avenues repeating themselves to the horizon;
clustered residential areas, once serving as suburban middle-class ref-
uges from the city but now absorbed into the urban mass. Stroll
through and see it up close. Notice the characteristic artifacts: department store, office building, warehouse, factory, chimney, boiler, elec-
tric pole, street mixing people with machines. For all the twentieth
century's new technologies and stylistic experiments, the apparatus of
everyday life still bears strong markings of the nineteenth century.

The same is true for many of our ideas and institutional arrangements. In the world of education, we still behave as though the effective way to prepare young intellects for the fight ahead were to divide
all youngsters of a certain age into groups of twenty or thirty, place
each group in a closed room with a somewhat older person, seat the
youngsters in rows of small desks, arrange for the older person to talk to
them for hours each day, have them write various sorts of exercises for

the older person to evaluate, and require them to speak periodically in class about the exercises they have written, about material they have read, about general issues the older person has raised. (Young people who survive a dozen years or so of that treatment often move on to the even stranger system of the lecture; there the older person gets to talk at them without interruption for fifty minutes at a time. **Very** nineteenth century!)

In these waning years of the twentieth century, the nineteenth century also keeps its hold on many ideas about social organization. In the analysis of social change, we cling loyally to ideas built up by nineteenth-century intellectuals. Intellectuals formed those ideas in their astonished reaction to what they saw going on around them: unprecedented concentrations of population, production, capital, coercive force, and organizational power. They formed ideas treating increasing differentiation as the master process of social change, ideas of societies as coherent but delicate structures vulnerable to imbalances between differentiation and integration, and other ideas connected to them.

The nineteenth-century incubus weighs us down. I hope this little book will serve as a lever to lift some of the burden. It addresses one big question: **How can we improve our understanding of the large-scale structures and processes that were transforming the world of the nineteenth century and those that are transforming our world today?** It asks in particular how comparisons among times, places, populations, structures, and processes can aid that understanding. It reviews a number of outstanding contributions to comparative analysis of big structures and large processes. On the way, it proposes accounts of national states, capitalist organization, urbanization, industrialization, and other big structures and large processes that often differ from conventional accounts. It enters a plea for historically grounded analyses of big structures and large processes as alternatives to the timeless, placeless models of social organization and social change that came to us with the nineteenth-century heritage.

Where did the old models come from? Before scholars codified them, practical people fashioned them to interpret their new, surprising nineteenth-century experiences. Let the nineteenth century speak.

"Machines are ruining all classes," declared Johann Weinmann in

1849. Weinmann, master stocking knitter in Erlangen, Germany, described the machine as "the destroyer of households, the ruination of youth, the inducer of luxury, the spoiler of the forests, the populator of the workhouse, and soon the companion of general upheaval" (Shorter 1969: 206). Weinmann was, of all things, sharing his thoughts with King Maximilian of Bavaria. In the shadow of 1848's revolution, King Max had established an essay contest on the topic of long-term remedies for material distress in Bavaria and in Germany as a whole. Weinmann's reply arrived with over six hundred others.

From Ansbach, for example, police official Carl Seiffert sent in remarks on a related worry: "Now while the rich replenish their ranks with moderation and are purely conservative, the lower classes are thriving only too greatly and an enormous proletariat is growing up that, if an escape valve is not opened, will soon demand to divide up the property of the wealthy" (Shorter 1969: 201). Although Seiffert did not share Weinmann's concern about machines, both writers feared the growth of a dissolute proletariat and warned of its threat to property and public order.

Three themes reverberated through the entries to King Max's contest: overpopulation, mechanization, and immorality. The middle-class essayists felt that heedless breeding of the proletariat, migration of surplus rural people, and the consequent rapid growth of cities were creating new dangers for political and moral order. Many of them felt that machines threatened humanity. They argued, furthermore, that the combination of overpopulation with mechanization dissolved old social controls, thereby promoting dissolution, rebellion, crime, and violence. Traditional ways were disintegrating. Or so they thought.

Honest nineteenth-century burghers found many things about their century puzzling and distressing: the rapid growth of cities, the mechanization of industry, the restiveness of the poor. Putting such things together, they created a commonsense analysis of social change and its consequences. That bourgeois analysis posited an unending race between forces of differentiation and forces of integration. To the extent that differentiation proceeded faster than social integration, or to the extent that integration weakened, disorder resulted.

What, in this formulation, qualified as differentiation? Urbanization, industrialization, occupational specialization, the expansion of consumer markets, increasing education—anything that seemed to compound the distinctions among people, the contact of unlike beings with each other.

What was integration? A sense of likeness, shared belief, respect for authority, satisfaction with modest rewards, fear of moral deviation— essentially a set of habits and attitudes that encouraged people to reproduce the existing structure of rewards and authority.

What, then, was disorder? At the **small** scale, popular violence, crime, immorality, madness. If urbanization, industrialization, and other differentiating changes occurred without a corresponding rein- forcement of the sense of likeness, shared belief, and so on, these evils would beset individuals and families. At the **large** scale, popular rebel- lion, insubordination, class conflict. Increasing education, the expan- sion of markets, occupational specialization, and other forms of differ- entiation would cause these dangers as well, unless respect for authority, fear of moral deviation, and related forms of integration developed simultaneously—or at least survived. At either scale, a victory of differentiation over integration produced a threat to bourgeois security.

Nor were master stockingers and police officials the only people to see a contest between differentiation and integration. Their analyses did not differ fundamentally from the position Freiherr vom Stein had taken when addressing the Westphalian Parliament in 1831. The Freiherr was ending decades of public life; he died later that same year. Stein spoke of the "danger developing with the growth in numbers and claims of the lowest class of civil society." "This class," he declared,

is forming in our cities out of a homeless, propertyless rabble and in the countryside from the mass of little cotters, squatters, settlers, marginals, and day-laborers. They nurture the envy and covetousness bred by various other ranks of civil society. The present condition of France shows us how seriously property and persons are threatened when all ranks on earth are made equal. Fidelity, love, religious and intellectual development are the foundations of public and personal happiness. Without such a base the clash of parties undermines every constitution. [Jantke and Hilger 1965: 133]

Population growth, according to this analysis, was swelling the danger- ous classes and therefore increasing the differentiation of classes as it spread the demand for equality. The mechanisms of integration—

"fidelity, love, religious and intellectual development"—failed before the onslaught. The recent revolution (of 1830) in France made the dire consequences all too plain. Differentiation overwhelmed integration, and disorder flourished.

At the end of his long public life, Stein's warning has its ironies. With his ally Hardenberg, after all, the Freiherr himself had initiated Prussia's steps toward the liberation of the peasantry, the relaxation of restrictions on the exercise of various trades, and the constitutional reforms instituted at the start of the century.

Indeed, great landlord General von der Marwitz was to complain a few years later that Stein himself had started "the war of the propertyless against property, of industry against agriculture, of the transitory against the stable, of crass materialism against the divinely established order . . ." (Hamerow 1958: 69). Because of the destruction of lordly authority over the rural population, thought Marwitz, paternal control within the rural household had dissolved, young rustics considered themselves anyone's equal, and youngsters "want nothing more than to leave their home towns as fast as possible, and to find the town with the least discipline, where the apprentice plays master at the inn. Thus it is no longer the best, but especially the worst and laziest, who go out into the world." (Jantke and Hilger 1965: 136). Suddenly we see the distinction between modulated conservative caution and genuine reactionary hysteria.

Yet they have a common theme. To Stein, Marwitz, and other nineteenth-century conservatives or reactionaries, contemporary social change—in particular, the growth of a masterless proletariat— *Conservative view* threatened to overwhelm the political and moral bases of public order.

The basic analysis, however, could take on tones ranging from radical to reactionary. As a radical, one could value the change greatly, identifying the rise of the working class with *die Sozialbewegung*, the Social Movement. As an anarchist, one could regard the *radical view* disorder itself—so long as it acted in the right direction—as creative force. As a social reformer and surveyor, one could argue that if the growth of a proletariat caused disorder it was not because of the dissolution of social bonds or the diffusion of envy, but because sheer misery caused despair, and despair caused desperate action. As a laissez-faire liberal, one could consider the growth of the proletariat inevitable; then one might accept misery and disorder as costs of progress, costs to be contained but never quite eliminated. As a conservative or reactionary, finally, one could value integration so much that **any** substantial change seemed threatening.

Thinkers Face Change

In all these views, a balance between the forces of differentiation and of integration determines the extent of disorder. Stein the reforming conservative and Proudhon the *anarchisant* socialist actually held similar commonsense analyses of social change and its consequences. In those analyses, they joined many of their nineteenth-century fellows. Consider Alexis de Tocqueville's famous summary of factors behind the French Revolution of 1848, as he set them down in 1850–51:

The industrial revolution which in thirty years had made Paris the chief manufacturing city of France and had brought within its walls a whole new mass of workers to whom work on fortifications had added another mass of unemployed agricultural workers.

The love of material satisfactions which, with encouragement from the government, agitated that multitude more and more, and fomented in it the democratic illness of envy.

Newborn economic and political theories which tended to make people think that human misery was a result of laws and not of providence, that one could eliminate poverty by changing the system of taxation.

The contempt in which the governing class, and especially those at its head, had fallen—contempt so deep and general that it paralyzed the resistance of even those who had the greatest reason for maintaining the power that was being overthrown.

The centralization which reduced the whole revolutionary action to seizing control of Paris and taking hold of the assembled machinery of government.

Finally, the mobility of everything—institutions, ideas, customs, and men— in a moving society which had been stirred up by seven great revolutions in less than sixty years, not to mention a multitude of secondary shocks. [Tocqueville 1978: 113–14]

Tocqueville's emphasis on government brought in elements that Freiherr vom Stein had neglected in 1831. Yet when it came to questions of mobility and integration, Tocqueville clung to the common-sense interpretation of social change and its consequences. In his thinking of 1848, industrial expansion and population mobility challenged the state's integrative power. In his opinion, the contemporary state had failed the test.

Out of such nineteenth-century reflections on capitalism, national states, and the consequences of their growth grew the disciplines of social science as we know them. Economists constructed theories of capitalism, political scientists theories of states, sociologists theories of those societies that contained national states, anthropologists theories of stateless societies. Each discipline bore marks of its birthdate; economists were obsessed by markets, political scientists concerned by citizen-state interactions, sociologists worried by the maintenance of social order, and anthropologists bemused by cultural evolution toward the fully developed world of the nineteenth century.

Nevertheless, all disciplines dipped into their century's evolutionary thinking to some degree. For all of them, increasing differentiation—as specialized production, as individualism, as interest groups, or as something else—took on the air of a general historical law. For all of them, increasing differentiation posed a difficult problem of social integration. The sense of evolution appeared clearly in the great sociological dichotomies: status and contract, *Gemeinschaft und Gesellschaft*, primary and secondary groups, mechanistic and organic solidarity.

What Was Happening?

Nineteenth-century European observers were not wrong to think that great changes were happening. For several centuries, industrial expansion had occurred mainly in small towns and rural areas. Rapidly multiplying capitalists had acted mainly as merchants rather than direct supervisors of manufacturing. Capital therefore accumulated more than it concentrated, as the proliferation of semi-independent producers in households and small shops accounted for most of the large increase in manufacturing. In that era of mercantile capitalism, the European population had been very mobile, but had moved mainly within regional labor markets or in great systems of circular migration. Although regional labor markets and long-distance circuits deposited a residue of migrants in cities, mortality, fertility, and migration combined to produce no more than modest urban growth. Indeed, many cities lost population when the pace of activity in their hinterlands slowed.

During the nineteenth century, in contrast, capital concentrated. Individual capitalists and firms acquired much greater masses of productive means than they had ever owned before. Capitalists took direct hold over the processes of production and located them increasingly near markets and sources of energy or raw materials instead of near supplies of self-sustaining labor. Production, rather than exchange, became the nexus of capitalism. Accordingly, the process of proletarianization that had long been at work in the countryside moved to the city. Large firms employing disciplined wage-workers in urban locations became increasingly important worksites. Workers migrated from industrial hamlets, villages, and towns toward manufacturing cities and industrial employment, as displaced agricultural workers moved into urban services and unskilled labor. Small wonder that Karl Marx, observing these very processes, should fix on the separation of labor from the means of production and the conversion of surplus value into fixed capital as virtual laws of nature.

As results of this urban implosion of capital, net rural-urban migration accelerated, cities increased rapidly, large areas of the countryside deindustrialized, and differences between country and city accentuated. Mechanization of production facilitated the concentration of capital and the subordination of labor. Sometimes, in fact, we write this history as the story of technical improvements in production. At its extreme, the technological account postulates an "industrial revolution" depending on a rapid shift to grouped machine production fueled by inanimate sources of energy and dates "industrialization" from that proliferation of factories, machines, and industrial cities.

Within manufacturing, the pace of technical innovation did accelerate during the nineteenth century. The spinning jenny, the power loom, and the blast furnace certainly increased the amounts that spinners, weavers, and smelters could produce in a day. Steam power, assembly lines, and factories evidently became crucial to many branches of industry after 1750. In all these regards and more, the nineteenth century made a technological break with its predecessors.

To call the nineteenth-century reorganization of production an "industrial revolution," nevertheless, exaggerates the centrality of technological changes. It draws attention away from the great transformation of relations between capital and labor that marked the century. It ignores the fact that in all industrial countries, including England, small shops predominated in almost all branches of production up to the start of the twentieth century. Not until the automobile era did time-disciplined, assembly-line factories become the characteristic sites of proletarian production. To date industrialization from the development of the factory, furthermore, relegates to nothingness centuries of expansion in manufacturing via the multiplication of small producing units linked by merchant capitalists. It also hides the vast deindustrialization of the European countryside that accompanied the nineteenth-century implosion of manufacturing into cities.

As capitalism was undergoing fundamental alterations, European states were likewise entering a new era. By the second half of the eighteenth century, national states had made themselves the dominant organizations in most parts of Europe. Their preparations for war had become so extensive and costly that military expenditure and payments for war debts occupied the largest shares of most state budgets. The strongest states had built great apparatuses for the extraction from their populations of the means of war: conscripts, food, supplies, money, money, and more money. Paradoxically, the very construction of large military organizations reduced the autonomy of military men and created large civilian bureaucracies. The process of bargaining with ordinary people for their acquiescence and their surrender of resources—money, goods, labor power—engaged the civilian managers of the state in establishing limits to state control, perimeters to state violence, and mechanisms for eliciting the consent of the subject population.

Those states, however, continued to rule indirectly. For routine

enforcement of their decisions, collection of revenues, and maintenance of public order, they depended mainly on local notables. The
notables did not derive their power or tenure from the pleasure of
superiors in the governmental hierarchy. They retained plenty of room
for maneuver on behalf of their own interests. As a result, much of the
business of national authorities consisted of negotiating with local and
regional notables. Ordinary people carried on an active political life,
but almost entirely on a local or regional level. When they did get
involved in national struggles for power, it ordinarily happened
through the mediation of local notables, or in alliance with them.

During the nineteenth century, all this changed. Although war kept
on getting more costly and destructive, it less often pitted members of
the European state system against one another and more often involved conquest outside of Europe. Revolutionary and reformist governments extended their direct rule to individual communities and
even to households. In the process of bargaining with ordinary people
for even greater resources, statemakers solidified representative institutions, binding national elections, and a variety of means by which
ordinary people could participate routinely in national politics.

Under pressure from their constituents, likewise, states took on re-
sponsibilities for public services, economic infrastructure, and household welfare to degrees never previously attained. The managers of
national states shifted from reactive to active repression; authorities
moved from violent reactions against rebellion and resistance as they
occurred toward active surveillance of the population and vigorous
attempts to forestall rebellion and resistance. All these activities sup-
planted autonomous local or regional notables and put functionaries
in their places. As a consequence, notables lost much of their strength
and attractiveness as intermediaries in the attempts of ordinary people
to realize their interests. Those were the nineteenth century's great
changes.

Big Structures, Large Processes, Huge Comparisons

Nineteenth-century Europe's great shifts in organization set the frame
for this book in two complementary ways. **First,** those shifts formed the
context in which our current standard ideas for the analysis of big

social structures, large social processes, and huge comparisons among social experiences crystallized. **Second,** they marked critical moments in changes that are continuing on a world scale today. Understanding those changes and their consequences is our most pressing reason for undertaking the systematic study of big structures and large processes. We must look at them comparatively over substantial blocks of space and time, in order to see whence we have come, where we are going, and what real alternatives to our present condition exist. Systematic comparison of structures and processes will not only place our own situation in perspective, but also help in the identification of causes and effects.

With capitalism and the state in rapid transformation, nineteenth-century European burghers, intellectuals, and powerholders had good cause to worry about social change. They made serious, even desperate, efforts to understand what was happening to them. Those efforts created the nineteenth-century conceptions which now encumber our thought.

From a mistaken reading of nineteenth-century social changes emerged the eight Pernicious Postulates of twentieth-century social thought. They include these principles:

1 "Society" is a thing apart; the world as a whole divides into distinct "societies," each having its more or less autonomous culture, government, economy, and solidarity.
2 Social behavior results from individual mental events, which are conditioned by life in society. Explanations of social behavior therefore concern the impact of society on individual minds.
3 "Social change" is a coherent general phenomenon, explicable *en bloc.*
4 The main processes of large-scale social change take distinct societies through a succession of standard stages, each more advanced than the previous stage.
5 Differentiation forms the dominant, inevitable logic of large-scale change; differentiation leads to advancement.
6 The state of social order depends on the balance between processes of differentiation and processes of integration or control; rapid or excessive differentiation produces disorder.
7 A wide variety of disapproved behavior—including madness, murder, drunkenness, crime, suicide, and rebellion—results from the strain produced by excessively rapid social change.

8   "Illegitimate" and "legitimate" forms of conflict, coercion, and
    expropriation stem from essentially different processes: processes of
    change and disorder on one side, and processes of integration and
    control on the other.

All eight are mistakes. Although national states do, indeed, exist,
there is no "society" that somehow exercises social control and em-
bodies shared conceptions of reality. Social behavior does not result
from the impact of society on individual minds, but from relationships
among individuals and groups. "Social change" is not a general process, but a catchall name for very different processes varying greatly in
their connection to each other. Stage theories of social change assume
an internal coherence and a standardization of experiences that disappear at the first observation of real social life.

The difficulties continue. Although differentiation is certainly one
important process of change, many of the fundamental changes in our
era actually entail dedifferentiation, and to some of them the question
of differentiation is secondary or even irrelevant. It is simply not true
that rapid social change produces generalized strain, which in turn
creates alternative forms of disorder as a function of the available
avenues of escape. The more closely we look, the more coercion by
officials resembles coercion by criminals, state violence resembles private violence, authorized expropriation resembles theft. We will return to these difficulties repeatedly later on.

The eight illusions connect neatly; they follow from a sharp division
between the forces of order and the forces of disorder:

	$+$	$-$
ORDER		DISORDER
society	——	individual mental event
integration	——	disintegration
satisfaction	——	strain
legitimate control	——	violence
progress	——	decay
normality	——	abnormality

These sharp dichotomies rest on a sense that social order is fragile, that
differentiation threatens social order, that change is risky, that unre-
strained change generates strain, violence, decay, and disintegration,
that only guided and contained change leads to integration, satisfac-

tion, and progress. They express the will of powerholders—actual or would-be—to improve the people around them, by means of coercion and persuasion, at a minimum cost. To the extent that they still promulgate these ideas, the social sciences of the twentieth century remain the bearers of nineteenth-century folk wisdom.

My summary exaggerates the unity of nineteenth-century thought. The opposition of order to disorder characterizes the teachings of Durkheim and Tönnies much more than those of Marx or Weber. Both Marx and Weber regarded a sort of order as all too likely. They thought it would take demonic force—of revolution or of charisma—to disrupt the existing order. But Marx and Weber stood far from nineteenth-century folk wisdom. Sadly, the lines of social-scientific thought that embodied folk wisdom prevailed well into the twentieth century.

[margin note: exaggerates unity of 19 c. thought.]

Fortunately, the social sciences that formed in the nineteenth century also took observation seriously. Much the same spirit that brought burghers and bureaucrats to worry about rising disorder induced social reformers and officials to undertake surveys of living conditions, establish household censuses, collect statistics, and publish documented descriptions of social life. In western Europe, the half-century from 1870 to 1920 was the golden age of official statistics and social surveys; after that period, official statistics and social surveys became more efficient and regular, but lost much of their richness. However faulty, the results of social inquiries set challenges to theories of social change; at a minimum, analysts had to explain away the contrary evidence. A combination of mutual criticism and accumulated evidence has made it clear that the eight great nineteenth-century postulates are illusions.

[margin note: 18 great 19th postulates are illusions— seen by evidence, statistics, etc.]

What to Do

If the notion of a contest between differentiation and integration fails us, if we cannot usefully reduce social behavior to the impact of society on individual minds, if the picture of the world as an ensemble of coherent societies, each undergoing similar processes of change in partial independence from the others, misleads us, if the analytic distinction between legitimate and illegitimate varieties of coercion blocks our comprehension of political processes, if there is no general phenomenon of social change whose sequences and consequences we can usefully model, much of the intellectual apparatus social scientists have inherited from the nineteenth century will not work. What should we do?

We should build concrete and historical analyses of the big structures and large processes that shape our era. The analyses should be **concrete** in having real times, places, and people as their referents and in testing the coherence of the postulated structures and processes against the experiences of real times, places, and people. They should be **historical** in limiting their scope to an era bounded by the playing out of certain well-defined processes, and in recognizing from the outset that time matters—that *when* things happen within a sequence affects *how* they happen, that every structure or process constitutes a series of choice points. Outcomes at a given point in time constrain possible outcomes at later points in time.

If the work is historical, it need not be grand. When it comes to understanding proletarianization, for example, much of the most valuable work proceeds at the scale of a single village. Keith Wrightson and David Levine's study of Terling, Essex, from 1525 to 1700 tells us more about the creation of a propertyless underclass than do reams of general essays about capitalism. Ted Margadant's analysis of the 1851 insurrection against Louis Napoleon's coup d'état has more to teach about the actual process of rebellion than dozens of broad statements about the pattern of revolt in Europe as a whole.

Nor, for that matter, need historical work concern the distant past. Take Arthur Stinchcombe's treatment of the durable influence of the "social technology" prevailing at the time of an organization's founding on its basic structure. Stinchcombe applies essentially the same analysis to the structures of industrial crafts, men's college fraternities, savings banks, trade unions, and other organizations. He shows both that organizations of a given type tend to be established in spurts and that the structures they adopt at the outset persist over long periods of time (Stinchcombe 1965: 153ff.). While the argument is eminently historical, it brings us right up to the present. A concrete, historical program of inquiry must include work at the small scale and can well include our own time.

In the case of Western countries over the last few hundred years, the program begins by recognizing that the development of capitalism and the formation of powerful, connected national states dominated all other social processes and shaped all social structures. The program continues by locating times, places, and people within those two master processes and working out the logics of the processes. It goes on by following the creation and destruction of different sorts of structures by capitalism and statemaking, then tracing the relationship of other processes—for example, migration, urbanization, fertility change, and household formation—to capitalism and statemaking. A demanding program, but a rewarding one.

This book makes only a small contribution to the program. For Western countries in recent centuries, it asks:

1   What fundamental large-scale processes must we distinguish in order to understand how that world has changed and is changing?
2   How do those processes relate to each other?
3   What social structures experience those processes?
4   How can systematic, large-scale comparison help us understand the structures and processes involved?
5   In approaching these questions, how much should we rely on the intellectual frames we have inherited from the nineteenth century?

In trying to answer these questions, I reason mainly from a series of outstanding works that have addressed them in recent years. Most of my examples come from sociology and political science. Those are the two fields of the social sciences that produce the largest volume of self-conscious large-scale, comparative research on social structures and processes. I regret my relative neglect of anthropology, economics, geography, and, especially, history. But each of them poses special problems deserving discussion by themselves. Some other time.

In aiming a small book at large questions, I have veered away from may problems other authors might reasonably take up under the headings "big structures, large processes, and huge comparisons." In the pages to come, you will find little discussion of the logic of comparison as such; "strategies for the comparative study of big structures and large processes" comes closer to my intentions. Although I discuss a number of specific writings, you will look in vain for a continuous, comprehensive history of thinking about big structures and large processes. You will find no reviews of previous works on comparative analysis;

little treatment of existing models of migration, population growth, capital accumulation, and other large processes; not much on techniques or evidence.

For the most part, I will resist the temptation to trot out examples of bad comparative analysis, like prisoners from their cells, for interrogation and shaming; many convicts languish deservedly in those cells, but they will stay in the dark. In compensation, the bibliography contains enough references on these matters for someone to start a campaign of systematic reading.

Do those omissions leave anything to talk about? Plenty, I think. First, a review of the eight misleading postulates we have inherited from nineteenth-century social science. Then, a discussion of various strategies for comparison of big structures and large processes. Along the way, observations and speculations on what actually happened in modern Europe.

The book's three elements dovetail nicely. Criticism of misleading nineteenth-century ideas leads effortlessly both to a search for comparisons to test and revise those ideas and to the formulation of alternative histories for the Western past.

2

FOUR PERNICIOUS POSTULATES

False Principles

The nineteenth century's legacy to twentieth century social scientists resembles an old house inherited from a rich aunt: worn, overdecorated, cluttered, but probably salvageable. Appraising the old structure, we will want to save the belief in intelligible patterns of social interaction, the hope that disciplined observation will make those patterns more intelligible, the search for fundamental structures and processes, the attempt to reconstruct the processes that created our contemporary ways of life, and the organization of these inquiries as a cumulative, collective enterprise. We will want to retain a few specific theories, such as Marx's theory of capital accumulation. But we will also want to throw out and strip down.

To reduce the clutter, false general principles derived from the bourgeois reaction to nineteenth-century changes should be the first to go. Let us discard the ideas of society as a thing apart and of societies as overarching entities; of social behavior as the consequence of individual mental events shaped by society and of those mental events as the links between persons and societies; of social change as a single coherent phenomenon; of standard stages through which societies develop;

of differentiation as the dominant, inevitable logic of social change; of a contest between differentiation and integration as the source of order and disorder; of disorder itself as a general phenomenon resulting from the strain of rapid social change; of sharp separation between legitimate and illegitimate forms of coercion, conflict, and expropriation.

In recent years, the eight pernicious postulates have lost some of their hold. The encounters of European and American social scientists with the Third World, with social scientists based in the Third World, and with critics of their own governments' involvements in the Third World have shaken all the postulates to some degree. In the 1950s, for example, international meetings of experts on Third World urbanization and industrialization almost always concluded that rapid change was increasing the likelihood of rebellion and protest in Third World countries, that the growing slums of Third World cities bred crime and disorder, that excessive migration to cities by people forced off the land was producing an explosive urban situation.

The summary report of a 1959 international seminar in Santiago, Chile, classified the "problems arising in modern countries as a result of the formation of an industrial society" as (1) dissolution without replacement of traditional structures; (2) appearance of contradictory social structures facing individuals with contradictory requirements; (3) excessively rapid changes, including those of mass rural migration. "Maladjustment reveals itself in the three classes," concluded the rapporteurs,

as a lack of norms, or anomy, in the individual. People's behaviour is always conditioned by a number of frames of reference which guide their actions, and their modes of feeling and thought. They may be the stricter norms of the traditional society or the more elastic criteria of choice which are typical of an industrial society. In any event, the individual needs adequate inner resiliency: the application of prescribed solutions or the manoeuvring of different selective criteria. During a period of transition, however, the individual may find himself deprived of one or the other. [Echavarria and Hauser 1961: 54]

The language is guarded, but the argument's lineaments come through clearly. In general, it conforms to the nineteenth-century postulates.

Turning to the comparable literature of the 1970s, I can hardly suppress a fantasy. What if the participants in the 1959 meeting had all fallen fast asleep (at the plenary session of an international conference, not an unthinkable event), only to wake up twenty years later, in the midst of another international conference? What a shock for them! Consider the proceedings of a 1978 conclave in Delhi: The reports and general statements bristle with ideas of dependency, of capitalist penetration, of survival strategies for the poor and powerless. "In summary," comments the volume's editor,

. . . capitalist penetration appears to shape the process of urbanization in the Third World in several distinctive ways. It leads to the eventual disintegration of the rural subsistence sector and increasing reliance on the urban informal economy; to increasing articulation between the formal and informal sectors of the urban economy; to increasing internal differentiation within cities, including differentiation within caste or ethnic groups; to increasing demands on the state for public services and infrastructure, while the autonomy of the state is simultaneously weakened by foreign intervention; and to the possibility of increased collective action and protest focused on the state by the urban poor who have continually been denied access to adequate housing, jobs, education and other necessities. This process has developed much further in Latin America, which has experienced a longer history of capitalist penetration than Africa or Asia, where in many areas it is just beginning. [Safa 1982: 13]

Some of the old words and problems remain; the discussion still features disintegration and differentiation. The vocabulary still includes plenty of debatable terms. Some of the shift merely attaches new labels to old theoretical baggage. Yet the basic orientation has changed. Ideas of anomie, maladjustment, overurbanization, and excessively rapid change have disappeared, while many participants take for granted that the most pressing theoretical problems are to connect local events to international structures of power and to improve existing models of those international structures.

Since the 1950s, in short, the classic themes have almost disappeared from scholarly discussion of changes in the Third World. In the meantime, a combination of theoretical criticism, political sensitization, and field research had brought the specialists to see structure everywhere: in what had once seemed pell-mell flight from the land, in the shantytowns of Latin America, in the Third World's popular politics.

Other fields have not altered their perspectives so radically. Students of crime, of fertility, of organizational structure, and of religion, awakening from the 1950s, would still have a good deal to discuss with their successors of the 1980s. Nevertheless, on the whole wherever specialists actually examine big structures, large processes, and huge comparisons the nineteenth-century postulates have lost their dominance.

Some postulates have lost more ground than others. The ideas of society and societies have come under strong attack from advocates of world-system analysis, but no theory or practice dispensing with them has really taken hold. Much social analysis still takes individual mental events, rather than social relationships, as the center of social life. Except among Marxist theoreticians, it has become unfashionable to fashion general statements about social change as such. Stage theories have lost much of their glitter, partly as a result of the move away from general theories of social change. Differentiation still captures the imagination of many social analysts, especially those who worry about fragmentation of everyday existence. The balder theories pitting differentiation against integration have given way to explanations of the same presumably "disorderly" phenomena as organized, interest-oriented behavior.

At the same time, scholars have become much more skeptical about the sequence rapid change/strain/disorder. Yet no comparable decline has struck the notion of two separate processes underlying "illegitimate" and "legitimate" coercion, conflict, and expropriation. In varying degrees of health, the eight pernicious postulates still live. Let us take them up in turn, giving more attention to those that currently play an important part in social scientists' theories of large-scale structure and process.

Society Is a Thing Apart

Sociology's greatest victory as an academic discipline brought its greatest defeat as an intellectual enterprise. Persuading others that a distinct realm called "society" and distinct entities called "societies" existed freed sociologists to justify their studies. Those premises justified sociology as at once essential and independent of philosophy, psychology, or biology. Although human beings created society, once in existence society had its own laws. Such presociological thinkers as Montesquieu had long since established the practices of comparing "societies" and of distinguishing between formal organizations (especially states) and the social structures, or societies, shaping and sustaining them. Comte, Spencer, Durkheim, and other nineteenth-century greats consolidated those practices into a discipline called sociology. That discipline promised to explain social variation and to develop means of repairing rents in the social fabric. On the basis of those promises its promoters built a method, an organization, and a cluster of concepts: society, norm, role, status, collective belief, and so on.

In the same process, a division of labor emerged. Sociology investigated the internal structure of rich, powerful societies. Anthropology, for its part, received a double duty: to account for large variations among societies and to analyze the internal structures of societies outside the charmed circle of power and wealth.

That accomplishment, nevertheless, gave sociologists and anthropologists a terrible burden: the task of delineating structures and processes of fictitious entities. As a practical matter, sociologists usually began with existing national states and defined society residually. Society was everything else but the state, or everything but the organization of production, the structure of distribution, and the state. As John Meyer and Michael Hannan say, a bit uneasily, in the introduction to their own studies of international inequalities:

Almost all these ideas have a common frame: there are entities called societies in which the hypothesized forces operate. Societies are internally interdependent systems, such that the transformation of one subsystem leads to the transformation of all the others. True, external factors operate at the boundaries of each society, generating market pressures, political threats and opportunities, and social and technical innovations. But once these factors impinge on a society, the main consequences occur through the internal structural processes that maintain the coherence of the society as a bounded system. Leave for later the defects of this perspective, which clearly takes too seriously as distinct units the national political states that are created and become dominant as a *product* of the history of modern development. [Meyer and Hannan 1979: 3]

Later on, as promised, they voice second thoughts. They wonder about the legitimacy of models and statistical procedures such as theirs, which treat the hundred-odd countries whose characteristics they correlate as coherent, independent entities (Meyer and Hannan 1979: 11–13). They have reason to doubt.

Anthropologists have customarily dealt with the problem of delineating societies either by starting with a local community and assuming that the definitions of identity with others stated by members of that community delineated a larger "society" or by accepting the political entities—"tribes," "peoples," "kingdoms," and so forth—encountered by westerners in the course of commercial and imperial expansion. They, too, have run into doubts. Many anthropologists who lean toward statistical analysis, for example, worry about "Galton's problem": the likelihood that as a result of diffusion of cultural traits adjacent "societies" fail to qualify as the independent cases one needs for crisp analyses of cultural covariation. (Galton's problem was no afterthought: E. B. Tylor announced Comparative Method as anthropology's new program at a meeting of the Royal Anthropological Institute in 1889; at that very session, in comments on Tylor's own paper, Galton raised this very objection; thus the difficulty has dogged the doctrine from its very beginning: Hammel 1980: 146–47).

Ethnographers who have observed the coexistence and interpenetration of distinctly different cultural identities, furthermore, despair of bundling the world up neatly into separate societies. Those separate, autonomous entities are fictitious.

All of the standard procedures for delineating societies run into severe trouble when the time comes either to check the clarity and stability of the social boundaries thus produced or to describe the coherent structures and processes presumably contained within those boundaries. How? In many variants, all the troubles return to two fundamental difficulties: **first**, how to make boundaries of the "same" unit consistent in time, space, and personnel; **second**, how to determine whether the proposed boundaries do, in fact, delimit a distinct and coherent social entity.

In the first case, each of the criteria—national state boundaries, local-community statements, westerners' politically derived definitions—groups heterogeneous populations, produces conflicting delineations of the terrains and populations involved, and/or encounters changes in the apparently relevant boundaries. What bounds, for example, should we place around "German society" at the moment in which Europe contained dozens of states whose populations were mainly German-speaking, in which the courtiers of those same states affected French, and in which the Habsburg empire included not only a substantial block of German-speaking subjects, but also millions of people speaking Czech, Rumanian, Serbian, Turkish, and twenty other languages?

What about German society at the moment in which Napoleon's troops had conquered substantial German-speaking populations and laid down the French state's administrative apparatus in important parts of Central Europe? German society at the moment in which Prussia and a number of other mainly German-speaking states formed a customs union, while emigrants from their territories had established numerous German-speaking communities in the Americas? German society in the days of the Federal Republic, the Democratic Republic, Berlin, and the Austrian Republic—not to mention German-speaking enclaves in Czechoslovakia, France, Switzerland, Italy, Hungary, and elsewhere?

No consistent set of boundaries will contain all these multifarious entities, or even their cores. No continuous German Society underwent all these permutations. German society, as such, did not exist.

The second problem is to delineate coherent, distinct social entities. Without some coherence and distinctiveness, one cannot reasonably treat a "society" as a self-sustaining entity with dominant norms, values, beliefs, and mechanisms of control. Yet we have no a priori guarantee that current national-state boundaries, local-community statements, or westerners' conquest-derived delineations—to return to the three standard means of identifying societies in sociology and anthropology—mark the limits of interpersonal networks, shared beliefs, mutual obligations, systems of production, or any of the other presumed components of a "society."

In principle, to be sure, we face an empirical question: To what extent do the boundaries of different kinds of social relations coincide? Certainly some geographic divisions separate a wide range of social life; consider the lines separating West Berlin from East Berlin, Haiti from the Dominican Republic, Hong Kong from the Chinese People's Republic. Surely national states control migration, trade, and many other flows across their frontiers. Unquestionably people on either side of the Hungarian-Austrian border see a boundary that bounds genuine differences.

Yet these politically reinforced frontiers do not contain all social life. Economic geographers enjoy demonstrating how different in scale and contour are the units defined by different activities or social relations: ties of credit versus ties of marriage, trips to buy food versus trips to sell computers, and so on. Economic geographers also delight in showing the enormous, even worldwide, extension of some sorts of interdependence: intercontinental migration chains, huge circuits of trade, far-flung professional structures, international flows of capital. Both demonstrations challenge any notion of neatly packaged social units.

Savor, for example, a geographer's final word on the notion of region:

In summary, regions do exist, they do have meaning, and we can delineate them. However, they are not clear-cut areas in which activities are confined. Rather, regions are useful more as a system of classification; they are imperfect generalizations of the underlying spatial complex, which itself can be better described as the connections of countless individuals, farms, plants, and businesses. [Morrill 1970: 186]

The point applies as well to regions at the scale of the national state or the continent as it does to smaller territories.

Although activities and populations have orderly spatial distributions, they typically lack sharp boundaries. Such boundaries as exist for one activity or population almost never coincide with the boundaries defined by another activity or population. (Anyone who tries to separate the area called "Canada" from the area called "United States" by means of communications flows, markets, personal acquaintance, and other criteria of interaction soon discovers how much social life spans the legal frontier. See Bourne and Simmons 1983: 45.)

If we insist on clinging to the idea of societies as spatial clusters, we have only a few choices: (1) to turn the existence of large, bounded, comprehensive, coherent social groups—of societies—from a general presumption to an empirical question: to what extent, and under what conditions, do such groups ever form?; (2) to choose a single activity or relationship—citizenship, language, market—as the criterion of a society's boundaries and leave the relationship of that phenomenon to the boundaries of other phenomena open to empirical inquiry; (3) to admit that social relations form continuous fields and to block out "societies" more or less arbitrarily within those fields.

Unless the world does, however, fall into neatly bounded complexes of friendship, kinship, production, consumption, power, belief, and language, any of the three procedures compromises the effort to erect within the boundaries of a "society" the norms, roles, beliefs, values, hierarchies, controls, and self-sustaining activities about which we presume to theorize. Even if every aspect of social life had its own sharp boundaries, that would not be enough. If boundaries of different sorts of action do not **coincide,** the idea of a society as an autonomous, organized, interdependent system loses its plausibility. Not all interdependent systems, to be sure, have sharp boundaries. But an interdependent system that is at once distinct from adjacent systems and organized around enforced rules requires such boundaries.

If a spatial criterion does not delineate societies, other criteria work even less well. We are therefore better off in abandoning the notion of "society" and "societies" as autonomous systems. We are better off in adopting the alternative idea of multiple social relationships, some quite localized, and some worldwide in scale.

In recent years, advocates of world-system analysis have been offering a similar critique of the notion of society, but concluding that the remedy is to consider the entire world a single unit of analysis. Easy in principle, hard in practice. So far, world-system analysts have had more success in pursuing the remedy theoretically and conceptually than methodologically. In fact, a number of the most visible empirical efforts inspired by world-system ideas—for example, those of Richard Rubinson and Christopher Chase-Dunn—have produced their evidence through statistical analysis of data for national aggregates. By introducing blockmodeling into analyses of the world system, David Snyder and Edward Kick have directly represented relations among national states as the objects of analysis. Their work offers one of the few indications that an alternative method is coming into view.

Having only one case to analyze certainly blocks the application of conventional procedures for the study of variation among independently observed units, while making time-series analysis difficult. But a single case has not kept geologists from extending our firm knowledge of the earth or biologists from building tolerable models of particular ecosystems. The most serious difficulty, in my opinion, lies in the shift to observation of **interactions** rather than the behavior of individual units. There is no inconsistency among conceiving of the world as a connected whole, testing whether the hypothesized connections exist, and examining numerous interactions to see whether they correspond to the expectations we derive from our models of that connected whole. But there we confront the legacy of the nineteenth century: Both existing evidence and ingrained habits of thought depend on the fragmentation of interactions into characteristics of individuals and of societies.

Paradoxically, the belief in societies as overarching social structures with their own logic dovetails neatly with the belief in the socially conditioned mental event as the prime link between person and society. A mind, in the simplest model, internalizes society and directs behavior in conformity with that internalization. Undesirable behavior then results from imperfect internalization or from a bad fit between what the mind internalizes and the immediate situation of the troubled individual.

Mental Events Cause Social Behavior

It is easy and convenient to think of individual mental events as (1) products of social life, (2) determinants of social behavior, (3) links between persons and societies. With that postulate, we can readily sum individual consciousnesses into a global mentality.

Social researchers have built a good deal of their twentieth-century technique on the assumption that individual mental events are their basic social units. The survey, our own time's dominant means of amassing evidence on social life, involves a direct attempt to stimulate and record individual mental events for aggregation into social structure. If we include censuses—the largest of all social surveys—individual interviews and questionnaires provide the great bulk of the hard evidence that social scientists analyze.

By and large, our techniques for deriving group structure from individual observations remain feeble and artificial. Standard techniques of computing and statistical analysis in the social sciences assume that the evidence refers to independent individual events; data-analysis routines work best when the evidence comes in uniform, separate individual packets; statistical models compare an observed distribution of individuals with the distribution of individual events produced by random processes or by an ideal type such as perfect equality or complete segregation. The practice of social scientists depends on a close analogy between the social behavior under study and the operation of an idealized market.

Yet just as real markets consist of shifting, constructed social relations among limited numbers of actors, other social structures begin with interactions among persons (see White 1981). When we discover that some of these interactions recur in approximately the same form, we can reasonably begin to speak of social structure. Rather than individual orientations, social ties. Rather than social atoms, social networks.

Let me state this delicate point with care. Individual human beings exist. No one can see, hear, smell, taste, or feel a social relationship in the same sense that he can identify another human being. Social relationships, indeed, are merely abstractions from multiple interactions among individual human beings. But that brings us to the point: We abstract not from individual behaviors, but from sets of individual behaviors involving two or more persons at a time.

If the point seems strange, consider two problems. First, how do we know that an individual encountered at several separate times is the "same" individual? Organisms, to be sure, persist form birth to death. Willfully scientific identifications of individuals depend on lasting features of the organism such as height, skin color, scars, fingerprints, dental structure, and facial configuration. Yet what we normally experience as sameness ultimately depends on the reckoning of relationships. Al remains Al as the son of Bill, the lover of Cathy, the father of Dorothy, the employer of Ed.

The ability to simulate or reconstruct such relationships, in fact, allows imposture: By falsely claiming the same set of relationships, one organism can assume the identity of another. In historical work, Ian Winchester points out, we can only reasonably say we have identified an individual when we have linked at least two different records referring to the same person. That record-linkage amounts to connecting the historical persons to the authors or recipients of the documents.

Second, what do a firm, a household, a patron-client chain, a lineage, a football team, and a community have in common? Surely not that they consist of some precise set of individuals, but that they amount to very different ways of organizing relationships among individuals. A player leaves, the team continues.

The point is not new. Forty years ago, Pitirim Sorokin was inveighing against the search for the "simplest social unit," and especially against the acceptance of the individual as the basic social unit. "The most generic model of any sociocultural phenomenon," wrote Sorokin, "is the meaningful interaction of two or more human individuals" (Sorokin 1947: 40. Rediscovery of those arguments in my old teacher's writings recalls one of Sorokin's preferred putdowns. "A very good idea, Mr. Tilly," he would rumble in his heavy Russian accent, "but Plato said it better.")

On the base of meaningful interaction, Sorokin built an elaborate taxonomy of social interaction, culminating in cultural "supersystems." The social sciences are, I think, better off for having abandoned the effort to construct complex, supposedly comprehensive classification schemes for relationships and groups. But the recognition that relationships are the basic social units did not deserve to die with the classification schemes.

Following an approach sketched long ago by Georg Simmel but strangely neglected by subsequent sociologists, Harrison White has fashioned this insight into a simple, effective instrument of social analysis. White begins with populations of two or more individuals and distinguishes a pair of elements: categories and networks. A population forms a **category** to the extent that its members share a characteristic distinguishing them from others. (White restricts his attention to characteristics that the persons themselves recognize as shared with the others, but his formulation adapts readily to common characteristics identified by outside observers.) All Welshmen, all coal miners, and all viola players are examples of populations qualifying as categories.

A population forms a **network** to the extent that its members are connected by the same social tie. The tie may be direct—from Alice to Boris, Alice to Celeste, and Boris to Celeste as well. It can also be indirect—from Alice to Boris and Alice to Celeste, but not from Boris to Celeste, a configuration that links Boris and Celeste via Alice. The chain of people who pass gossip or rumors defines a network that is often not a category. So does the web of debts among people who have borrowed money from one another.

A population forms a **catnet** (category x network), finally, to the extent that both conditions—common characteristics and linking ties—apply. A catnet, thus described, comes close to the intuitive meaning of the word "group." Nuclear families, households, firms, voluntary associations, churches, states, armies, and parties, among other sets of persons, commonly meet the criteria for a catnet. Whether those entities we refer to indecisively as communities, institutions, classes, movements, ethnic groups, and neighborhoods correspond to genuine catnets remains an empirical question: Some do, some don't. Societies, cultures, civilizations, peoples, publics, and masses, as analysts ordinarily use these words, almost never qualify as catnets. Indeed, in most cases the words do not even designate bounded populations, categories, or networks.

The elementary units of categories, networks, and catnets are not individual mental events, but relationships: relationships established by the sharing of social characteristics on the one hand and by the presence of social ties on the other. By specifying the character and intensity of the social characteristics and/or social ties in question, we can accomplish three fundamental tasks of social description:

1 establish workable taxonomies of social structures for particular analytical purposes;
2 convert absolute distinctions such as community/noncommunity into empirically distinguishable continua;
3 locate observable sequences of human behavior within the taxonomies thereby established.

Thus we may identify a specified population as a household **to the extent that** its members share a distinct dwelling and food supply, and collaborate in the maintenance and use of the dwelling and food supply.

Such a definition immediately brings out similarities and differences between a household and a barracks, a prison, a hospital, a hotel, or a picnic ground. It also allows variation as to the degree of distinctiveness in dwelling and food supply or the extent of collaboration among household members. With the elementary apparatus of population, relationship, category, and network, the basic tasks of social description become manageable.

In eschewing socially conditioned mental events as the prime ties of individuals to societies, must we also abandon rational-action models of social behavior? No, we need not jettison the life preserver with the ballast. In many fields of social inquiry, models of social behavior as rational choice offer our best hope of escape from the tyranny of societal determinism. What we need, however, is better means of moving from the action of a single person or group taken in isolation, to rational **inter**action among two or more actors.

Take the study of social movements as a case in point. In understanding contemporary social movements, rational-action models of the kind proposed by William Gamson have much greater explanatory power than the society-driven irrationalism that so long dominated the study of crowds, protests, and movements. To use rational-action models, we have no need to assume that all collective action is fundamentally calculated, willed, desirable, feasible, and efficacious. We need only assume, provisionally, a coherent set of relationships among the interests, organization, shared beliefs, and actions of the actors. Rational-action models of social movements generally assume a single actor—a movement, organization, an aggrieved group, or something of the sort—provide accounts of that actor's behavior, and sometimes state the effects of that behavior.

Rational-action models typically call for a specification of the actor's decision rules and current values for the elements of those decision rules. The elements ordinarily include (1) costs of different possible courses of action, (2) benefits of those possible courses of action, (3) capacity of the actor to bear the costs of alternative actions. Thus we explain participation in a social movement as the outcome of individual choice among possible courses of action whose relative attractiveness depends on a multiple: (estimated benefits − estimated costs) × (capacity to act). The actor may be an individual or a group. Still other actors enter the analysis chiefly as objects of action or constraints rather than as living participants in the social movement.

There the trouble begins. Real social movements actually consist of sustained interactions among authorities and challengers. Within real social movements, various challengers attempt to create a coherent actor, or at least its appearance. Furthermore, real social movements always involve a symbolically constrained conversation among multiple actors, in which the ability to deploy symbols and idioms significantly affects the outcome of the interaction. Existing theories and models do not provide useful accounts of that interaction.

Game theory provides one possible way out. It extends individual decision-making to the analysis of interactions, via radical simplification of the alternatives and of time; in general, each action ends and has a visible outcome before the next action begins. The simplification makes it feasible to treat both simultaneous action by two or more parties and mutual consideration of the other's action.

Robert Axelrod's work with the Prisoner's Dilemma shows the value of that simplification. In its elementary form, the Prisoner's Dilemma results from a two-person interaction in which self-serving action by both parties produces an undesirable outcome (such as staying in jail) for both, cooperative action by both parties produces a more desirable outcome (such as shortened jail terms) for both, but self-serving action by one coupled with cooperative action by the other produces a highly desirable outcome (such as getting out of jail immediately) for one party and a highly undesirable outcome (such as a lengthened jail term) for another. Many real-life situations have properties of the Prisoner's Dilemma: environmental pollution, arms races, legislative trade-offs, and even the natural encounters of potentially symbiotic organisms (Axelrod and Hamilton 1981). In a single encounter of these kinds, both parties have strong incentives to avoid cooperation and serve themselves.

Yet if the parties interact frequently, the situation changes. Over repeated interactions, even entirely egoistic actors tend to gain from strategies combining initial cooperation with a sharp discrimination of subsequent responses depending on whether the other party cooperates or serves himself. TIT FOR TAT—I begin by cooperating in the first encounter and do whatever you did last time in subsequent encounters—tends to win over all strategies that are more self-serving in the short run. The advantage of an initially cooperative strategy increases with (1) the likelihood of subsequent encounters, (2) the sharp discrimination of responses, and (3) the certain identification of the other party, his actions, and their consequences.

Even in the midst of a population of inveterate self-servers, further-more, a small cluster of tit-for-tat aficionados tends to win out. (Axel-rod's results bear a striking resemblance to Mancur Olson's analysis, in *The Rise and Decline of Nations*, of the likelihood that small groups and groups having access to selective incentives will form advanta-geous "distributional coalitions.") Axelrod's theoretical and experi-mental results immediately suggest real-life analogies to legislative log-rolling, military and diplomatic alignments, and collusion among corporations. The analogies, in their turn, suggest the possibility of generalizing game-theoretical approaches to big structures and large processes.

Jon Elster has recently suggested just that. "By assimilating the principles of functionalist sociology, reinforced by the Hegelian tradi-tion," he announces, "Marxist social analysis has acquired an appar-ently powerful theory that in fact encourages lazy and frictionless thinking. By contrast, virtually all Marxists have rejected rational-choice theory in general and game theory in particular. Yet game theory is invaluable to any analysis of the historical process that centers on exploitation, struggle, alliances, and revolution" (Elster 1982: 453).

Borrowing from Arthur Stinchcombe, for example, Elster proposes an application to revolutionary situations: Revolutionary action be-comes likely when, in the presence of vulnerable powerholders, poten-tial opponents to those powerholders communicate with each other sufficiently to recognize that they have the collective capacity to over-turn the existing structure. The Assurance Game—which resembles Axelrod's TIT FOR TAT—tends to replace the Prisoner's Dilemma. The process of starting up the game has something in common with the milling that commonly occurs at the start of a risky collective action: Participants are collecting information about the likelihood that other people will defect instead of sticking with the action; if much of the information reads "defect," even determined veterans often call off the demonstration, raid, or occupation. So long as strategic interac-tion forms a significant part of the process at hand, game theory offers a promising way to shift from individual mental events toward social relationships without losing the precision of rational-action analysis.

Nevertheless, game theory will not suffice. Eventually we must find the means of placing relationships rather than individuals at the very center of the analysis. Many of the relationships that constitute and constrain social life have so small a component of strategic interaction as to require other sorts of analysis. Communication networks, routine relations between bosses and workers, flows of tax money, spread of diseases, movements of capital, chain migrations, and promotion ladders all certainly involve strategic interaction at one time or another. But their crystallization into durable structures requires a specifically structural analysis. So, for that matter, does their incessant change.

"Social Change" Is a Coherent Phenomenon

It would be astounding to discover that a single recurrent social process governed all large-scale social change. Perhaps the hope of becoming the Newton of social process tempts social scientists into their repeated, fruitless efforts at discovering that philosopher's stone. Newton, however, had some concrete regularities to explain: the acceleration of falling bodies, the behavior of celestial objects, and many others. Social scientists are not so lucky. At Newton's level of empirical generality—that of the world or the universe as a whole—they have no significant and well-established uniformities to explain.

Somehow the absence of an explicandum has not kept social scientists from elaborating general models of social change. Nor has it kept them from using social change in general as a cause of other phenomena: social movements, emotional distress, crime, suicide, divorce.

Their quest is idle. There is no such thing as social change in general. Many large-scale processes of change exist; urbanization, industrialization, proletarianization, population growth, capitalization, bureaucratization all occur in definable, coherent ways. Social change does not.

In recent years, I must admit, few social scientists have said otherwise. Among the rare exceptions are Robert Hamblin, Brooke Jacobsen, and Jerry Miller. They have published A *Mathematical Theory of Social Change*. The theory itself treats all change as innovation and diffusion. Their social change has two main variants: creation of a new social form whose use then spreads; modification of an existing social form, whose modification then spreads. They then allow for two processes of diffusion: one with persuasion, the other without it.

Hamblin, Jacobsen, and Miller put the theory into mathematical form as a specification of the time-shapes of diffusion under varying conditions. Their Theorem 1, for example, presents the time-shape of diffusion where the adoption is potentially unlimited, persuasion is operating, and adoption results in differential reinforcement among users. In those circumstances, by their reasoning, the relevant equation is:

$$\frac{dU}{dt} = ae^{kt}$$

where dU/dt is the rate of adoption, k is an empirically derived estimate of the "level of energy input into the system," a is a scaling constant, and e is the base of Naperian logarithms (Hamblin, Jacobsen, and Miller 1973: 200). In short, this portion of the theory says that when an innovation of positive value to all users spreads in an unlimited population via persuasion, the rate of adoption will increase exponentially. In similar situations where the potential users are limited, they expect the rate of adoption to describe a logistic curve. And so on. They are able to fit exponential curves quite closely to periods of acceleration in air passenger miles traveled on U.S. carriers, motor vehicle registration, gasoline consumption, higher degrees granted in the United States, marriages and divorces, production and possession of television sets, and several other items.

In further efforts, Hamblin, Jacobsen, and Miller fit logistic, decaying exponential and other curves to series representing behavior they claim to be appropriate to the different variants of their basic models. They also develop and estimate arguments about the relationships among rates of scientific discovery, industrial productivity, investments in education and research, and industrial investments. Again, they focus on the time-shapes of the relationships and do their curve-fitting empirically. Having finished, they suggest that eight of the relationships they have identified amount to scientific laws (Hamblin, Jacobsen, and Miller 1973: 214).

Why, then, have these results stirred so little interest among students of social change? Perhaps because numerate social scientists already knew that a number of diffusion processes followed logistic, exponential, and other regular patterns, while the rest knew too little of the relevant mathematics to recognize the discovery.

The Hamblin-Jacobsen-Miller theory itself, however, suggests another explanation: Specifications of the time-shapes of diffusion were
not what students of social change needed; therefore they did not adopt
them. The explicandum needs more than precision to make it interesting. It must also connect to the Big Questions: Why do poor regions
stay relatively poor, why did capitalism radiate from western Europe,
under what conditions do ordinary people rebel, what causes persistent
inequality among races and sexes, what conditions promote tyranny,
when and why do wars occur, and on down the standard checklist.
Even in a day of scientism, the social sciences have not—
hallelujah!—lost their ultimate concern with the fate of mankind.

The worst version of the belief in social change as a coherent general
phenomenon, from the viewpoint of practical effects, is its implicit
version, the version built into standard methods without requiring any
reflection of their users. Three variants come to mind. The first is the
use of comparison among a large number of units—most often national states—at the same point in time as the means of drawing
conclusions about **sequences**: for instance, drawing conclusions about
"political development" by arraying a hundred countries all observed
in 1960 to 1970 along a scale established by means of a multiple
regression of numerous variables for each of those countries. There is
no logical connection between the sequence of change in those variables followed by individual countries and the differences that show up
in a cross-section. Worse yet, there is no logical justification for the
scale itself; although multiple regression and similar techniques will,
indeed, show which characteristics covary in linear fashion, that
covariation is as likely to result from diffusion or from common structural position in a worldwide system as from any internal logic of
development.

Longitudinal inferences from cross-sectional comparisons occur so
widely in the social sciences that it is a bit unfair to single out an
instance to illustrate my complaint. With apologies to the authors for
discriminatory treatment, let me choose an otherwise well-conceived
piece of research. Jacques Delacroix and Charles Ragin examine the
claims of modernization theorists and their critics by means of a comparison of 49 poor countries in 1953 and 1965.

Interested in the impacts of various presumably modernizing institutions on economic growth, Delacroix and Ragin test alternative ac-

counts of change in Gross National Product/Capita from 1950 to 1970. Their dependent variable, then, puts longitudinal data into play. From a reading of Alex Inkeles and David Smith on modernization they derive the expectation that higher secondary school enrollments and cinema attendance will lead to greater increases in GNP/capita. From their own reflections on Alejandro Portes' criticism of modernization theories they draw the predictions that (1) schooling will have a positive effect on GNP/capita, while exposure to American movies will have a negative effect; (2) "countries with mobilizing regimes should be characterized by stronger positive effects of the school and weaker negative effects of the cinema than countries with non-mobilizing regimes" (Delacroix and Ragin 1978: 131). Accordingly, they introduce a dummy variable representing their own classification of the forty-nine states as mobilizing or nonmobilizing.

On the basis of further arguments, Delacroix and Ragin represent the possible effect of world-system position by the proportions of 1953 imports that were finished goods and the proportion of 1953 exports that were raw materials. Inserting a control for initial level of wealth, they estimate a series of equations in the form:

$$\log_{10}(\text{change in GNP/capita } 1950\text{--}1970) = A + BY_{tl} + C_i Xi_{tl} + U_{tl}$$

where A is a constant, B and C_i are regression coefficients, U_{tl} is an error term, Y_{tl} is level of wealth in 1950, and Xi_{tl} are the independent variables in 1953.

Delacroix and Ragin use the 1965 levels of schooling and of cinema attendance only to establish that their increase after 1953 is independent of the level of GNP/capita in 1950. They interpret the regression estimates as casting doubt on the "modernization" theses and supporting the Portes-inspired dependency alternative: positive effect of schooling, negative effect of Western cinema, stronger positive effect and weaker negative effect in mobilizing regimes, no effect of total cinema attendance, and so on.

I would not be surprised if the Delacroix-Ragin conclusions were correct. But you can't get there from here! Let us suppose, for example, that the positive association between levels of schooling at the beginning of a period and the extent of economic growth during the period held up through a wide variety of samples, measures, and specifications of the model. That association would still be compatible with any of the following interpretations:

1   Increases in schooling do, indeed, promote economic growth.
2   Economic growth promotes increases in schooling.
3   Increases in schooling are unrelated to economic growth, but level of schooling and current rate of economic growth both depend on extent of previous contact with rich countries.
4   Increases in schooling are unrelated to economic growth, but economic growth is now in the early stages of a long-term diffusion from countries with high levels of schooling to countries with lower levels of schooling.
5   A temporary wave of economic growth is in the late stages of propagation from countries with **low** levels of schooling to countries with high levels of schooling.

If the dependent variable had been static (as it often is in such analyses), even a wider range of interpretations would have been consistent with the evidence.

To some extent, Delacroix and Ragin could make each of these more or less credible by inserting new variables into their cross-sectional analysis. So long as their presumed causes act in multiple countries at the same point in time, however, such analyses can never provide strong evidence for one standard sequence or another. It would serve the Delacroix-Ragin logic much better to move directly to longitudinal evidence; in the first crude step, to estimate whether **changes** in the level of schooling in a given period predicted to changes in GNP/capita in a later period. A cross section provides no substitute for a time-series.

The second variant compounds this difficulty. It consists of using factor analysis or similar techniques to take many, many characteristics of separate "societies" and reduce them to a few "dimensions" of variation. In a venerable example, Philip M. Gregg and Arthur S. Banks factor-analyzed sixty-eight variables included for an unstated number of "political systems" indexed in the Banks and Textor *Cross-Polity Survey*. They extracted seven statistically independent dimensions, which they labeled **access, differentiation, consensus, sectional-**

ism, **legitimation, interest,** and **leadership. Differentiation,** for
example, included strong positive or negative loadings on the following variables:

POSITIVE	NEGATIVE
period of political modernization	charisma
date of independence	aggregation by executive
westernization	ex-French dependency
articulation by associational groups	unicameral legislature
semimodern bureaucracy	articulation by nonassocia-
ex-Spanish dependency	tional groups
bicameral legislature	developmental ideological
later European political modernization	orientation
conventional ideological orientation	African areal grouping
elitism	post-colonial bureaucracy
aggregation by legislature	undeveloped tutelary political
	modernization

Let us slide past the meaning of these "variables," which deserve
discussion on their own. Banks and Gregg say of this dimension that its
extremes "contrast late stages of modernization against undeveloped
tutelary modernization, conventional against developmental ideology,
semimodern against postcolonial bureaucracy, and aggregation by
legislature against aggregation by executive" (Banks and Gregg 1971:
297). Noting that the extremes do not contrast westernized democracies with traditional monarchies, they conclude that the dimension
represents only a portion of the entire continuum of political development: the "differentiation of political institutions within former colonial dependencies" (Banks and Gregg 1971: 297).

The placement of their hundred-odd states within a sequence of
development, however, is gratuitous; it assumes precisely what must be
proven: that the arcs of change in individual states follow the pattern of
their cross section in the 1960s. If we began with a theory specifying
the power of a limited number of underlying variables, and then
selected the characteristics to be analyzed in accordance with their
logical correspondence to the underlying variables, a factor-analytic

approach might possibly make sense. As a procedure for discovering relationships, it is hopeless.

The third variant is, alas, the most common. It consists of estimating relationships among variables all aggregated to a national level, but actually representing observations on a wide variety of social units: presence or absence of a bicameral legislature (observed directly for national state), urbanization (aggregated from local populations), Gross National Product (aggregated from market transactions), median age (aggregated from individuals), proportion of labor force in agriculture (aggregated in peculiar ways from households and/or firms), and so on. Leave aside the great faith in the quality and comparability of the data such a procedure entails. To have any confidence in estimated relationships among such diverse variables requires tremendous confidence either in the integrity of the national state as a coherent aggregate or in the generality and coherence of social change.

An otherwise excellent analysis of national fertility levels illustrates the problem. William R. Kelly, Dudley R. Poston, and Phillips Cutright seek to measure the impact of national population policies on fertility in "30 developed populations with more than one million inhabitants in 1965" (Kelly, Poston, and Cutright 1983: 95). They estimate relationships both cross-sectionally and as change from 1958 to 1978; thus they avoid having to make longitudinal inferences from cross-sectional comparisons. So far, so good.

Kelly, Poston, and Cutright estimate the effects of a number of population-policy and "development" variables by means of ordinary least squares regression. The predictor variables include:

- a development index giving equal weight to standardized versions of:
    percentage literate in 1970 population 15 and over
    newspaper circulation per 1000 population, 1970s
    life expectancy, 1970
    natural log of telephones/capita, 1970
    natural log of GNP/capita, 1970
    natural log of energy consumption, 1970
    proportion of population living in urban areas, 1970
- percentage of total labor force female, 1970s

- percentage of women 20–24 in marital or consensual unions, 1970s
- divorce rate, 1970s
- four-point scale for restrictiveness of [presumably national] abortion policy, mid-1970s
- three-point scale coding extent of [presumably national] population policy in terms of pronatalist/other policy and presence or absence of public or private family-planning clinics, mid-1970s
- proportion of married couples of reproductive age practicing contraception, mid-1970s (from sample surveys)

Fertility they measure as the Total Fertility Rate in 1958 and 1978. Among these variables, Kelly, Poston, and Cutright find that "development" predicts to contraception and to the presence of population policy, but not to female labor force participation. Fertility in 1958, contraception, the presence of population policy, and female labor force participation, in their turns, "predict" to declines in fertility from 1958 to 1978 and to differences among the thirty populations in 1978.

All that is plausible and may well be true. But look at the measurements: Although they do not have the heterogeneity of the caricature I offered earlier, they refer to (1) the population 15 and over, (2) the total population in the 1970s, (3) an aggregation of the population over some previous period (hidden in the computations of life expectancy), (4) the labor force, (5) women aged 20–24, (6) couples of reproductive age, and (apparently) (7) the national state. To lock these various units together in a causal analysis implies either an unstated theory of their interdependence or a belief in the generality of social change.

In the last analysis, all three variants of methodological naiveté result from the same basic problem. The available analytical procedures—from simple cross-tabulation to factor analysis—assume variation (1) among well-defined independent units in (2) independently observed characteristics of those units along (3) dimensions that are analogous to those built into the procedures. They also typically assume (4) that their user is estimating a well-specified model rather than exploring for statistical relationships. Rare is the study of large-scale structural change that meets even two of these assumptions halfway. The belief in social change as a coherent general phenomenon compromises the four crucial assumptions.

Stage Theories

Social scientists once used stage models of social change as freely as blacksmiths use their hammers; they banged away at almost every object that came into their hands. Models of economic or political development normally specified the stages through which every developing society had to pass, explained the movement of societies from stage to stage, and sorted the world's contemporary states into the postulated stages.

Stage theories of economic growth or of political modernization had many attractions. They were easier to construct, understand, and apply than were continuous multivariate models. When illustrated with existing states, they had a concrete realism that abstract models of change lacked. They provided a splendid organizing principle for comparative economic or political history. One could even imagine using a valid stage model to guide public policy toward countries at different phases of a common process. An all-purpose hammer, indeed.

During the last few decades, nonetheless, social scientists have packed away that well-worn tool. The general abandonment of optimistic development theories in the face of political criticism, of empirical disconfirmation, and of the elaboration of counter-theories featuring dependency and/or world-economic processes hastened the discarding of stage theories. So did the difficulty of forcing real national states, with their cantankerous complexity, into a single stage of development: What did one do with a Kuwait, oil-rich and dominated by a single lineage? With a South Africa, riven by division between poor blacks and prosperous whites? With a Turkey, a large share of whose workers were off earning money in Germany or Switzerland?

For that matter, even the effort to fit the historical experiences of the classic European cases into standard stages fell on hard times. The last volume of the famous Studies in Political Development, for example, compared the United Kingdom, Belgium, Scandinavia, the United States, Spain, Portugal, France, Italy, Germany, Russia, and Poland—not to each other, but to a well-known stage model. At that point in its career, the Committee on Political Development, sponsor of the volume, was using a flexible five-stage scheme. The scheme called for a developing state to solve five crises, those of Identity,

Legitimacy, Participation, Penetration, and Distribution. The scheme's authors were no longer confident that the crises fell into a regular sequence. They allowed for the possibility that crises overlapped in time, but thought the sequence in which a developing country resolved those crises might well stamp its subsequent political life.

In this last fling, the Committee on Political Development invited a group of specialists in the histories of these various countries to prepare analyses treating the character and sequence of the five crises in each of the countries. Even in such a soft version of a stage theory, however, the historians could barely oblige. They had trouble identifying the crises and more trouble trying to date them. They used different definitions of crises and different criteria for sequences. Despite that delinquency—or perhaps because of it—they wrote reflective, useful essays.

Whatever else they accomplished, the essays did not confirm the scheme of five well-defined crises. As Raymond Grew, the volume's editor, reported,

The concept of "crises" being "resolved" has faded; one is merely looking at problems that at a given moment are (or seem) more or less pressing. For better or worse, most of the crises we emphasize have long held their place in historical tradition, and the sequences deduced from them are relative more than absolute, a chronology of salience more than clear sequence. [Grew 1978: 14]

Thus the most attenuated version of the most carefully prepared of all stage schemes for political development failed to order the historical experience. The scheme wrote its own obituary.

Why? Both histories and historians resisted the forcing of complex events into simple, abstract categories. The histories did, in fact, display some common properties and problems: the establishment of military control over their territories, the organization of fiscal systems, the negotiation of representation for the people who supplied the troops and paid the taxes, the cooptation or subordination of churches, and so on. In that weak sense, the scheme of crises (now conceived of as an inventory of major problems faced by statemakers) survived. But the lesson of those common properties and problems is not that another version of an abstract stage model would work well. It is that making the inquiry genuinely concrete and historical also helps to make the experience intelligible.

3

FOUR MORE PERNICIOUS POSTULATES

Differentiation Is a Progressive Master Process

No doubt the marked successes of evolutionary models in natural history encouraged nineteenth-century social theorists to adopt differentiation as a master principle of social change. The specialization of work, the subdivision of governments, the extension of commodity markets, and the proliferation of associations all seemed to exemplify rampant differentiation. The invention of the simple, undifferentiated, "primitive" society as a model of the small, poor populations Europeans encountered in the course of their mercantile and colonial expansion articulated neatly with the same scheme. All societies fell on the same continuum from simple to complex, differentiation drove societies toward greater and greater complexity, and complexity created strength, wealth, and suppleness. The fittest—the most differentiated—survived.

To be sure, differentiation always had rivals. Auguste Comte placed the advance of knowledge at the base of long-term social change;

mankind progressed from Theological to Metaphysical to Positive society through the accumulation of sure, disciplined, and comprehensive scientific understanding. Karl Marx saw changes in the organization of production, broadly defined, beneath the carapace of politics and culture. Nevertheless, within the disciplines of the social sciences, two nineteenth-century hypotheses hardened into twentieth-century dogmas: first, that increasing differentiation was the dominant, nearly inexorable logic of large-scale change; second, that over the long run differentiation leads to advancement.

After World War II, theories of "modernization" and "development" epitomized the social-scientific concern with differentiation as the fundamental large-scale social process. All such theories took the world's rich and powerful countries to be more differentiated than other countries, considered that differentiation to constitute a significant part of their advantage over other countries, and held out the creation of new, specialized structures as a major means by which poorer and less powerful countries could come to share the comforts of the rich and powerful. These theories connected closely with an improving program, a program of deliberately inducing development. Both theories and program, in their turn, rested on an optimistic ideology.

The ideology, as F. X. Sutton has reminded us, involved three central tenets: "(1) the capacity of governments as agents and guides to development; (2) the efficacy of education and training; and (3) the possibility of mutually beneficent cooperation between rich and poor countries in an equitable international order" (Sutton 1982: 53). Early United Nations programs of aid to poor countries embodied the ideology and promoted the spread of the associated theories; for all their cantankerous variation, academic specialists in development shared a certain confidence in the three tenets. They took on the mission of building theories that would simultaneously explain and guide the development of one country after another.

All such theories established a continuum of societies having rich Western countries at one end; they were, obviously, "modern" and "developed." Economists had the easiest time of it. For many of them, development came to mean increasing national income, or income per capita. Whatever one could say about the difficulties of measuring national income accurately and in comparable terms, as a criterion of development national income had splendid virtues:

1 Properly measured, it provided a principle on which all countries could be ranked with little ambiguity.
2 Those countries which economists generally regarded as most advanced unquestionably stood at the top of the scale.
3 Countries in all parts of the world were moving up the scale with few important reversals.
4 Position on the scale clearly (if imperfectly) correlated with international power, material well-being, and a great deal more.

With that imperfect correlation, however, the troubles began. For political scientists, sociologists, anthropologists, and others took on the job of specifying, measuring, explaining, and even promoting the other changes that presumably accompanied rising national income. Political development, communications development, educational development, and a dozen other forms of development came into being. A new vocabulary proliferated: developing countries, underdevelopment, late developers, and so on.

Whatever other virtues these multifarious criteria of development had, none of them matched national income in simplicity or efficacy: International rankings remained quite arguable, odd countries kept showing up near the tops of the relevant scales, the continuous drift of the world's countries in the same direction was hard to establish, and the correlations among different presumed forms of development left something to be desired. Yet the nagging correlations persisted. It was somehow true, on the average, that richer countries had higher life expectancy, larger shares of their population in cities, greater literacy, smaller completed family sizes, more durable institutions of parliamentary government, and so on, through a long list of national characteristics not deducible by definition from national income.

Why? Although some people confused the idea of "modernization" with an answer, the word came to stand for a question: **Why** do these many characteristics vary together, but only imperfectly? Do they all spring from some underlying condition, such as the emergence of a certain kind of attitude or motivation, an alteration in the basic forms of production, or a revolution in communications? Or do they form a partly interdependent web of variables, such that a change in any of them induces changes in the others? So-called theories of moderniza-tion typically combined (1) the assertion that societies fall into a con-tinuous scale of advancement, (2) a proposal for description and mea-surement of two or more aspects of that advancement, and (3) an argument concerning the nature of the connections among those as-pects of advancement.

Daniel Lerner, one of the architects of modernization theory, defined modernization as "the social process of which development is the economic component" (Lerner 1968: 82). "We orient our definition in this sense," he went on to say,

in order to focus attention upon the proposition that is central to the analysis presented in this paper: namely, that there is a single process of modernization which operates in all developing societies—regardless of their colour, creed, or climate and regardless of their history, geography, or culture. This is the process of economic development, and since development cannot be sus-tained without modernization, we consider it appropriate to stress this com-mon mechanism underlying the various faces of modernization. [Lerner 1968: 82]

Lerner's curiously circular definition led him to work out from eco-nomic growth to changes he regarded as essential to economic growth: a shift from agriculture to manufacturing and services, urbanization, educational expansion. From there he proceeded to mobility, includ-ing "psychic mobility." Along the way he invoked the nineteenth-century schema of development from community to society. Lerner eventually arrived at a total transformation of social life, a total trans-formation having much in common with what Durkheim called the creation of organic solidarity: differentiated individuals constituting a society through the mediation of mass communication.

Thus Daniel Lerner, like many other theorists of modernization, ultimately appealed to the logic of differentiation—required and im-pelled by economic growth—as the fundamental process of change. On the model of specialization in markets and in the evolution of species, it became the key to transformation. What is more, it became a **progressive** process: In general and in the long run, increasing differ-entiation meant social advance.

In the course of his forty years as a theorist, Talcott Parsons carried on a love/hate affair with the analysis of differentiation. He began the very first page of his vast *Structure of Social Action* with a quotation from Crane Brinton: "Who now reads Spencer? . . . We have evolved beyond Spencer" (Parsons 1937: 1). In 1937, Parsons thought that Spencerian ideas, with their unilinear evolution, their utilitarianism, and their positivism, were dead; they had expired in the crossfire from Pareto, Durkheim, Weber, and other contributors to the Action Frame of Reference.

Late in his career, nevertheless, Parsons began to use analogies with organic evolution quite explicitly. In 1966, Parsons wrote that "a major feature of the evolutionary process is that progressively greater differentiation increasingly frees the cybernetically higher factors from the narrow specifics of the lower-order conditioning factors, thus enabling the basic patterns of the cultural system to become more generalized, objectified, and stabilized (Parsons 1966: 114). "If human 'history' consisted," he declared a few years later,

of a population of essentially unique "cultures," as has been alleged, this consideration would indeed virtually eliminate the relevance of "comparative method." But empirically, this simply is not the case; history consists rather, like the system of organic species, of an immensely ramified "inverted branching tree" of forms at many levels of system reference.

What ties the "branches," forms and levels together into a macro-system, is in the first instance common genetic origin. This is to say that differences among subsystems have, by and large, arisen through processes of differentiation from what in some sense have been "more primitive" forms. The human socio-cultural universe is by no means so variegated as, at least superficially considered, the organic seems to be, but it is by no means narrowly constricted. [Parsons 1971a: 102]

The argument does not return to Spencer, but it has a much more Spencerian tone than a reader of Parsons' 1937 declaration could have expected. In these passages, Parsons makes differentiation the fundamental process of change and the key to social advancement.

To the extent that we **identify** advancement with differentiation, to be sure, the progressive effect of differentiation becomes true by definition. Parsons tried to escape the tautological trap by treating enhancement of adaptive capacity as the test of evolution. He offered the United States, the Soviet Union, and Japan as the most "developed" societies by this criterion (Parsons 1966: 3). He did not, however, lay out the rules for judging adaptive capacity. His actual choices suggest that international power played the largest part in his own judgments of adaptive capacity. That criterion shows up behind his selection of the United States, the USSR, and Japan as "most developed" in 1966. (Why not Sweden? Switzerland? Canada? Iceland?) It also appears in Parsons' assignment of particular populations, past and contemporary, to his three levels of evolution: primitive, intermediate, and modern.

Much of this is nineteenth-century evolutionary thinking in a new garb. And it is wrong. Not that differentiation is an unimportant feature of social processes. Many significant social processes do involve differentiation. But many social processes also involve dedifferentiation: Linguistic standardization, the development of mass consumption, and the agglomeration of petty sovereignties into national states provide clear examples. Futhermore, differentiation matters little to other important social processes such as capital concentration and the diffusion of world religions. Indeed, we have no warrant for thinking of differentiation in itself as a coherent, general, lawlike social process.

Suppose we take the case for differentiation as the master process at its strongest, in the industrialization of nineteenth-century Europe. If we look at old crafts such as shoe production, with the mechanization and concentration of the nineteenth century we do witness subdivision of tasks and specialization of shops in different products and markets. That much seems like general differentiation.

To look only at new firms, however, biases the whole picture. In leather, textiles, and other major industries, the growing nineteenth-century firms actually succeeded, on the average, by concentrating their production on a very limited variety of cheap, standardized goods. If we looked only at those firms and the competition among them, we might believe that product differentiation underlay the whole process. But the new firms drove out higher-priced producers in small shops and households who had been producing a great variety of goods under widely varying conditions.

For centuries, a web of small entrepreneurs had linked those dispersed producers to national and international markets; those webs contracted and atrophied as the small entrepreneurs moved into other activities. Villages and mountainsides had hummed with industry; their households had pieced together incomes from farming, gardening, migratory labor, domestic service, and home manufacturing. Now they lost population, gave up industry and much of their trade, became almost exclusively agricultural. They dedifferentiated. In places where capital and labor concentrated, these changes had the air of differentiation. Outside those places and in Europe as a whole, differentiation declined.

In any case, summing up these massive changes in terms of differentiation or dedifferentiation distorts their fundamental character. After several centuries in which manufacturing grew—and grew substantially—through the multiplication of small, dispersed units linked by merchant capitalists, the nineteenth century brought a great movement of capital concentration. Capitalists accumulated capital as never before; converted it from variable to fixed by building or buying such expensive items as factories, steam engines, and locomotives; gained control of the labor process, established time- and work-discipline within spaces they controlled, extended wage-labor as the principal condition for involvement of workers in production; and concentrated their workers at a limited number of production sites.

From a geographic point of view, Europe felt an enormous implosion of production into a few intensely industrial regions, as capital, labor, and trade drained from the rest of the continent. Karl Marx, witnessing these changes, saw that employers used differentiation of tasks as one of their techniques for increasing their own control over production and undermining the power of workers. But he also saw that the fundamental process involved concentration rather than differentiation.

My point is not that concentration of capital, or concentration in general, is the fundamental social process. One could equally make the case for connection, or communication, or control of energy. Here is the point: In this abstract sense, no process is fundamental. In a given era, specific historical processes dominate the changes occurring in a given population or region. Over the last few hundred years, the growth of national states and the development of capitalism in property and production have dominated the changes occurring in increasing parts of the world. More generally, alterations in the organization of production and of coercion have set the great historical rhythms.

In other eras, the creation or decline of empires and the establishment or destruction of command economies have dominated all other changes. Those historically specific changes in the organization of production and coercion, rather than abstractly specified processes such as differentiation or concentration, mark out the limits for intelligible analysis of social processes.

Differentiation Versus Integration

A belief in differentiation as the master process of social change clamps neatly to a nearby postulate: that the state of social order depends on the balance between processes of differentiation and processes of integration or control, with rapid or excessive differentiation producing disorder. Rapid or excessive differentiation, in this view, produces disorder. Differentiation can take the form of industrialization, urbanization, immigration of people from alien cultures, and any number of other changes. In essence, any change that increases the variety of social forms having durable connections to each other qualifies as differentiation.

Integration (alias social control, hegemony, and solidarity in different versions of the theory) can occur through repression, socialization, mutual obligation, or consensus. Disorder sometimes appears in this formulation as crime, as war, as emotional disturbance, as rebellion, as alienation, as family instability, as violence. Order, in most statements of the argument, amounts simply to the absence of disorder. In its classic version, the argument looks like this:

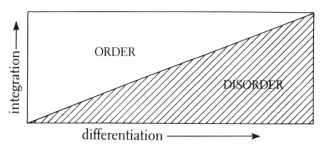

Thus if differentiation exceeds integration, disorder results. This reasoning leads to three somewhat different explanations of disorder:

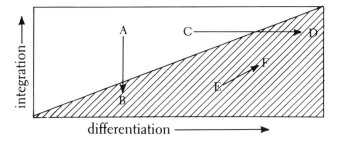

AB represents the first case: When integration declines, disorder occurs. CD describes the case in which differentiation proceeds without
a corresponding increase in integration; again disorder results. Finally
EF represents anarchy, where disorder continues to prevail because a
sufficient level of integration never appears.

Arguments of this type slide easily into tautology. To make the
argument circular, all we need is to define disorder as a certain kind of
differentiation and to define order as the absence of disorder. Thus if
the development of class conflict is at once a form of differentiation
and a variety of disorder, then class conflict occurs because differentiation exceeds integration. Class conflict occurs, in the tautological formulation, because class conflict grows too great for a society's integrative forces.

Nevertheless, differentiation-integration-disorder models sometimes
escape tautology. Take the idea that rapid urbanization uproots many
people from stabilizing social settings and places them in settings
where they have few controlling social ties and therefore engage in
antisocial behavior. That idea is dubious, but it is not tautological.

This classic line of argument will survive for some time, because it
articulates well with folk wisdom and political rhetoric alike. In one
version or another, it remains a standard explanation of urban problems, of crime, of divorce, of rebellion. True, it no longer enjoys the
unquestioned acceptance of a few decades ago; specialists in many
fields have erected alternatives to the differentiation-integration-
disorder scheme. In criminology, for example, theories of labeling, of
class conspiracy, of differential association, and of rational action have
all arisen as rivals to the once-dominant theories of social disorganization.

In the study of conflict and collective action, likewise, rivals to the
classic argument have appeared. On the whole, the reformulations
emphasize one or both of two ideas: that solidarity, rather than

insufficient integration, provides the necessary conditions of collective action, and that rebellions, protests, collective violence, and related forms of action result from rational pursuit of shared interests.

Writing about collective political violence in particular, Harry Eckstein has grouped the competing ideas under the headings "contingency" and "inherency." By and large, advocates of the differentiation-integration schema consider collective violence to be contingent, a result of some sort of aberration in the political process. Nonviolence is normal, violence abnormal. By and large, their critics lean toward an interpretation of collective violence as inherent in political life, as a by-product of routine struggles for power. "Contingency theories," remarks Eckstein,

of collective violence pivot on the notion of systemic breakdown where homeostatic devices normally provide negative entropy. It has been pointed out, correctly, that this implies sharp discontinuities between routine and nonroutine political activity, that the cause of violent action must be discontinuous (rapid, extensive) change in the context of politics, and that collective and individual behavioral pathologies should significantly covary, the former being a "version" of the latter. [Eckstein 1980: 144]

Eckstein considers almost all the contingency theories worth mentioning to be variants of relative-deprivation arguments, in which a discrepancy between people's expectations and their experiences motivates them to strike at others. Although he deplores the recent tendency of theorists on both sides of the line to elaborate their models instead of returning to first principles, on balance he considers that the evidence reported so far favors contingency rather than inherency.

Anthony Oberschall has another opinion. His division of ideas on social conflict into breakdown-deprivation theories and solidarity-mobilization theories corresponds roughly to Eckstein's contingency versus inherency. He describes breakdown theories as pointing to:

the dissolution of traditional social formations and communal solidarities as a result of rapid social change. Social disorganization, demographic pressures, and ecological imbalance lead to the accumulation of strains, frustrations, insecurity, and grievances, and the resulting pressure cooker has a tendency to explode in collective violence and civil disorders. After a time, processes of integration take the upper hand. Individuals become incorporated into new social formations and associations. Strain decreases, and grievances are pursued through regular institutional channels.

For breakdown theorists a sharp discontinuity exists between collective violence and more institutionalized forms of political conflict. The two forms of conflict require different conceptualization and theory. Breakdown theorists stress the similarity between the roots of collective violence and other forms of deviant and anomic behavior such as crime, mental illness, and suicide. They emphasize the marginality of participants in collective violence. They expect conflict to locate in growing industrial centers where anomie prevails, or else in weakened, disorganized rural communities. Frequently, they see collective violence as irrational tension release rather than as purposeful collective action to defend or obtain collective goods. [Oberschall 1978: 298]

As an active participant on the solidarity-mobilization side of this debate, I have trouble donning the robe of an impartial judge. But I must recognize that the debate remains open. Although evidence has built up against most of the assertions Oberschall puts into his inventory of breakdown theories, no solidarity-mobilization theory offered so far has the empirical backing to sweep the field. It is still possible, in principle, that a sophisticated contingency argument, involving actors cognizant of their rights and interests but beset by extraordinary circumstances, will turn out to explain collective violence and other varieties of conflict better than any argument treating violence and conflict as routine by-products of political life.

If that happens, however, the sophistication involved will still undermine any appeal to the tension between differentiation and integration. A sophisticated contingency argument treats conflict as the outcome of a certain kind of integration—at least within each of the parties to conflict—and thereby makes it more difficult to argue that uprooting, dissolution of controls, or individual disorganization have anything to do with the matter.

Change, Strain, Disorder

Oberschall's inventory likewise calls attention to another false postulate: the equivalence of different forms of disorder. Generations of social scientists clung to the nineteenth-century equation of crime, violence, family instability, rebellion, social movements, and other

forms of disapproved behavior. The equation made them all into disorder, disorganization, maladaptation. Various disapproved behaviors
became equivalent in several senses: (1) as direct evidence of the
malfunctioning of individual and society, (2) as consequences of rapid
and/or excessive social change, (3) as alternative expressions of the
same tensions, (4) as "social problems" to be solved in collaboration by
powerholders and social scientists. These equations coincided in an
extended version of the differentiation versus integration argument in
which rapid or excessive structural change built up a variety of strains,
and those strains expressed themselves in a range of disorders.

In the heyday of developmental theories, many theorists considered
these various forms of disorder to be unavoidable costs of development.
S. N. Eisenstadt put it this way:

The very fact that modernization entails continual changes in all spheres of a
society means of necessity that it involves processes of disorganization and
dislocation, with the continual development of social problems, cleavages
and conflicts between various groups, and movements of protest, resistance to
change. Disorganization and dislocation thus constitute a basic part of modernization and every modern and modernizing society has to cope with them.
[Eisenstadt 1966: 20]

It would be hard to find a purer specimen of the standard argument.

Fortunately, students of development often launched empirical inquiries in presumably disorganized areas. Those students sometimes
included natives of the areas under analysis. Now and then they came
to identify themselves politically and morally with the people whose
behavior was being explained. Under these circumstances, evidence
began to arrive concerning the various forms of order hidden in all that
presumed disorder. Studies of African and Latin American rural im-
migrants, for example, showed repeatedly the creation of rural outposts
in cities through chain migration, rather than the atomization, culture
shock, and consequent social disorganization the breakdown theories
required.

By the late 1960s, the reports on Third World urbanization reaching
semiofficial congresses on the subject had a schizophrenic air: report-
ing widespread organization where disorganization was supposed to
occur, but continuing to use the language of disorganization. We can
see a fine example in the vast report of a meeting on "urban agglomer-

ations in the states of the Third World" convened in Aix-en-Provence in 1967. The general reporter on Latin America, Gino Germani, noted that "a well known aspect of urban marginality is illustrated by the proliferation of shantytown, bidonvilles and the like. Problems of social disorganization among the migrants are well-known. However, in many cases, some social integration has also been maintained in the city through the transfer and adaptations of rural patterns" (Germani 1971: 748). The general reporter on Asia, C. N. Vakil, enumerated a series of physical and service deficiencies of Asian cities that were growing rapidly and added that "along with this, evils of urbanisation also show their ugly head—juvenile delinquency, prostitution, and problems of law and order and so on" (Vakil 1971: 943). The "are well known" and the "and so on" hide a growing contradiction between doctrine and evidence.

Ten years later, Joan Nelson evaluated the "theory of the disruptive migrants" on the basis of the accumulating evidence from throughout the Third World. Here is what she found:

In sum, the more dramatic and dire predictions about migrants' social assimilation are wide of the mark. The social mechanisms of family and home-place circles, sometimes supplemented by ethnic-group or voluntary associations or both, ease the transition and provide continuing social support for most migrants. That some are isolated, disappointed, desperate, is undeniable and should not be ignored. That others live as "urban villagers" in tight enclaves that turn their backs upon the city is also true, although much of what has been interpreted as evidence of "urban rurality" may be the result of superficial observation or misinterpretation. But the bulk of migrants in the cities of Africa, Asia, and Latin America are not isolated, disappointed, or desperate, nor are they urban villagers. Much of their lives, their aspirations, and their problems are shaped more by the pressures and the opportunities of the city than by their migrant status, and these pressures and opportunities are shared with urban natives of similar economic and educational background. [Nelson 1979: 108]

Little of the new evidence, I must admit, bears directly on the question of equivalence: When families do break up and youngsters do become thieves, do the same circumstances cause both outcomes? I think not, but definitive evidence has not yet come in.

Meanwhile, the rest of the structure lies in ruins. The sequence going from (1) rapid or excessive social change and dissolution of social control or support to (2) generalized distress, tension, or normlessness to (3) disorganization or disorder in general, expressed in a variety of undesirable behaviors—that sequence has proved an abysmal predictor of the actual course of Third World social change.

Illegitimate Versus Legitimate Force

All the pernicious postulates assume sharp separation between the worlds of order and disorder. The most explicitly political application of that assumption separates illegitimate and legitimate forces from each other. Illegitimate conflict, coercion, and expropriation, in this mystification, include riot, rebellion, assault, protection rackets, robbery, and fraud; they result from processes of change and disorder. Legitimate conflict, coercion, and expropriation, then, include war, crowd control, capital punishment, imprisonment, taxation, and seizure of property for debt; all of them presumably result from processes of integration and control. The very same acts, indeed, switch from illegitimate to legitimate if a constituted authority performs them. Killing appears in both columns, but with very different values. The values depend on whether the killer is a soldier, a policeman, an executioner, or a private person.

In the realm of politics, the distinction between illegitimate and legitimate uses of force is absolutely crucial. I don't deny its political necessity or the likelihood that I will call the police if someone steals my wallet or assaults my child. Nevertheless the sharp distinction should never have entered the world of systematic explanation. It is at once impractical and obfuscating.

The distinction is **impractical** because nearly identical actions fall on both sides of the line, and only a political judgment separates them. Recent attempts to build systematic theories of terrorism, for example, have foundered repeatedly over a simple fact: one person's terror is another person's resistance movement. Martha Crenshaw, who attempts to build from a neutral definition of terrorism, despairs of Conor Cruise O'Brien's normative approach: "He defines terrorism," comments Crenshaw, in terms of the political context in which it occurs, seeing terrorism as unjustified violence against a democratic state that permits effective and peaceful forms of opposition. Thus a black activist who bombs a police station in South Africa is not a terrorist; the Provisional Irish Republican Army (IRA) bomber of a British military barracks is. Identical acts performed in different situations do not fall under the same definition. [Crenshaw 1983: 1–2]

For theoretical purposes, such a criterion is impractical indeed.

The distinction between illegitimate and legitimate force is **obfuscating** because it reinforces the idea of a struggle between differentiation and integration and it separates phenomena that have much in common and spring from similar conditions. A small example comes from the study of collective violence: In the examinations of "riots" that proliferated with the great ghetto conflicts of the United States in the 1960s, it became customary to gauge the intensity of the event, among other ways, by the number of killed and wounded, to focus the analysis on explaining the participation of civilians in those riots, and to seek the explanation of variations in "riot intensity" in relationships among local social structure, selective participation of certain types of ghetto-dwellers, and the forms of action of the "rioters." In short, observers built their explanations as though the use of "illegitimate" force were a self-contained phenomenon, explicable through the character and circumstances of the people who used it and quite independent of the "legitimate" force deployed to stop it.

Small wonder, then, that no satisfactory explanations emerged: In fact, the events in question typically began with contested actions of police, the conflict consisted mainly of interactions between armed authorities and civilians, the armed authorities did most of the killing and wounding, and the extent of killing and wounding depended at least as much on the tactics of police and troops as it did on the number of people in the streets or the amount of property seized and destroyed.

Part of the confusion resulted from the use of the term **riot** itself. Like the words disturbance, mob, and rabble, the word belongs exclusively to authorities and hostile observers. Unlike demonstrators, participants in social movements, and vigilantes, people whom others call rioters never use the term for themselves. In Anglo-Saxon law, the term riot has long had legal standing. It denotes an assembly which frightens the public and, in the eyes of the authorities, displays the intention to break the law. After due warning and a decent interval for voluntary compliance, to declare an assembly riotous justifies the use of public force to disperse it. As a legal device, one can see why authorities find it useful. As an analytic term, however, it cuts through the very middle of the social interaction constituting the event to be explained.

A large example comes from the close analogy, rarely noticed, between racketeering and routine government. Both depend on the establishment of a near-monopoly of force in a given area and its use to coerce people to pay for goods or services offered by suppliers allied with the wielders of force and to exclude other suppliers of those goods and services from the market. To the extent that a government manu-factures external threats to justify the military protection it provides and the taxes it collects for that purpose, it operates a protection racket. Notice what happens when a sharp-eyed economist—no anarchist, he—takes up the analysis of racketeering:

> We can distinguish altogether three kinds of "monopoly": those achieved through legal means, those achieved through means that are illegal only because of anti-trust and other laws intended to make monopoly difficult, and monopolies achieved through means that are criminal by any standards—means that would be criminal whether or not they were aimed at monopoliz-ing a business. It is also useful to distinguish between firms that, in an excess of zeal of deficiency of scruple, engage when necessary in ruthless and illegal competition, and the more strictly "racketeering" firms whose profitable mo-nopoly rests entirely on criminal violence. The object of law enforcement in the former case is not to destroy the firm but to curtail its illegal practices. If the whole basis of success in business, though, is strong-arm methods that keep competition destroyed or scare it away, it is a pure "racket." [Schelling 1967: 63]

Schelling's distinctions, ironically, strengthen the analogy; they do not depend on any difference in the behavior of the monopolizers, but on the response of lawmakers to the monopolizers. Government is that racket which has managed to establish control over the most concen-trated means of coercion in an area and to command the acquiescence of most of the population to its use of those means throughout that area.

I don't insist on the strong word **racket** and certainly don't claim that the monopolization of coercion and the extraction of various forms of tribute exhaust the activities of governments. Nevertheless, notice how the analogy with racketeering clarifies the actions of governments we regard as illegitimate and the process by which new governments or quasi-governments arise.

Anyone who has looked closely at the formation of national states in Europe has seen elements of the process over and over:

- the early uncertainty as to the location of **the** government in the midst of great lords and private armies;
- the intense campaigns of kings and ministers to tear down castle walls, disarm the lords, diminish the private use of armed force in such forms as dueling and banditry, disband the private armies, incorporate all troops into forces under royal control, and turn nobles into royal military officers;
- the creation of distinct government-controlled police forces;
- the use of that growing monopoly of force to collect taxes, conscript soldiers, force the sale of salt, define and discourage smuggling, seize control of criminal and civilian justice, subject the population at large to registration and surveillance, regulate all other organizations.

Those processes **created** the distinctions between legitimate and illegitimate, legal and illegal, that exist today. Those distinctions and their origins are important objects of study. But as analytical distinctions, they do little but obscure the understanding.

Let that stand as an epitaph for all eight of the pernicious postulates the social sciences inherited from the nineteenth century. Without exception, they call attention to important processes, processes that frightened our nineteenth-century forebears, processes that remain influential today. Without exception, they construe those processes in such a way as to hinder their systematic analysis. We must hold on to the nineteenth-century problems, but let go of the nineteenth-century intellectual apparatus.

4

COMPARING

Eradicating Pernicious Postulates

How can we eradicate the pernicious postulates? Two approaches, one direct and the other indirect, promise to do the job. Directly, we should track the beasts to their dens, and battle them on their own grounds. We should look hard at the logical and evidential bases for generalizations about social change, about the use of illegitimate force, about differentiation as a master process. We should confront them with real historical cases and alternative descriptions of what actually went on. They cannot resist these weapons.

The **indirect** approach makes it easier to discover appropriate historical cases and to devise alternative explanations. It consists of fixing accounts of change to historically grounded generalizations. I do not mean universal statements confirmed by a wide variety of instances in different eras and parts of the world; at that level of generality, we have so far framed no statements that are at once convincing, rich, and important. I do mean statements attached to specific eras and parts of the world, specifying causes, involving variation from one instance to another within their time-place limits, and remaining consistent with the available evidence from the times and places claimed.

Big structures, large processes, and huge comparisons enter the analysis at precisely this point. They provide the stanchions to which we lash our historically contingent statements. Analyses of structures and processes operate at four historical levels, all of them involving comparison. At the **world-historical** level, we are attempting to fix the special properties of an era and to place it in the ebb and flow of human history. Schemes of human evolution, of the rise and fall of empires, and of successive modes of production, operate at a world-historical level.

At the **world-systemic** level, we are trying to discern the essential connections and variations within the largest sets of strongly interdependent social structures. World-system analyses, strictly speaking, certainly qualify, but so do Toynbee-style studies of civilizations. At the **macrohistorical** level, we seek to account for particular big structures and large processes and to chart their alternate forms. At the **microhistorical** level, we trace the encounters of individuals and groups with those structures and processes, with the hope of explaining how people actually experienced them.

Need I warn that the distinction of exactly four levels, rather than three, five, or some other number, leaves great room for debate? Unless we have compelling evidence that some kinds of large structures persist, cohere, and constrain all the rest, the number of levels between the history of a particular social relationship and the history of the world remains arbitrary. We should resist the temptation to reify the levels. I place the number at four on the wager that through most of history the world divided into at least two largely independent networks of production, distribution, and coercion. Our own single-network era began when the network of production, distribution, and coercion centered in China became inseparable from its counterpart centered in Europe.

If so, we can reasonably distinguish among analyses of (1) variation from network to network, (2) the operation of particular networks, (3) variation among structures and processes within particular networks, and (4) clusters of experience that people within particular networks treated as having common properties. Those define four levels: world-historical, world-systemic, macrohistorical, and microhistorical. If the world forms but a single coherent network, then the first two levels collapse into one. If the only significant uniformities and variations among structures and processes are those identified by the participants themselves, the distinction between the last two levels dissolves.

How many levels exist and what units define them are partly empirical questions. Within limits, we can amass evidence for or against Toynbee's claim that great civilizations, defined by people's interdependent involvement in a distinctive system of cultural premises, constitute the largest intelligible units of historical analysis. Within limits, we can also bring evidence to bear on the claim that at a certain point in time—including our own time—the entire world formed but one such system.

Adjudication of the evidence, however, requires agreement on the practical definitions of difficult terms such as "coherence" and "interdependence." If **any** connection counts, we will most likely discover that with trivial exceptions the world has always formed a single system. If only the sort of coherence nineteenth-century analysts attributed to societies counts, we will most likely discover that no system has ever existed. Somewhere between those extremes lie all useful accounts of human connectedness.

A sensible rule of thumb for connectedness might be that the actions of powerholders in one region of a network rapidly (say within a year) and visibly (say in changes actually reported by nearby observers) affect the welfare of at least a significant minority (say a tenth) of the population in another region of the network. Such a criterion indubitably makes our own world a single system; even in the absence of worldwide flows of capital, communications, and manufactured goods, shipments of grain and arms from region to region would suffice to establish the minimum connections. The same criterion, however, implies that human history has seen many world systems, often simultaneously dominating different parts of the globe. Only in the last few hundred years, by the criterion of rapid, visible, and significant influences, could someone plausibly argue for all the world as a single system.

Which structures and processes are crucial, then, depends on the level of analysis: world-historical, world-systemic, macrohistorical, or microhistorical. At the **world-historical** level, the main structures about which we are likely to make meaningful general statements are world systems. We are unlikely to fashion useful world-historical statements about households, communities, or even states, since the uniformities in their structure and variation are specific to one world system or another. The relevant processes for analysis at the world-historical level are the transformation, contact, and succession of world systems; at that level, generalizations concerning urbanization, industrialization, capital accumulation, statemaking, or secularization will probably collapse in the movement from one world system to another.

If we choose to work at this vast level, the comparisons we must undertake are comparisons among world systems—the hugest comparisons of human affairs. Personally, my eyes falter and my legs shake on this great plain. Others with stronger eyes and firmer legs are welcome to try the terrain. I don't believe, in any case, that we have established any well-documented and valuable general propositions at the world-historical scale.

At the **world-systemic** level, the world system itself continues to operate as a significant unit, but so do its major components, big networks and catnets defined by relations of coercion and/or exchange. Networks of coercion sometimes cluster into states: relatively centralized, differentiated, and autonomous organizations controlling the principal concentrated means of coercion in delimited spaces. Networks of exchange sometimes cluster into regional modes of production: geographically segregated and interdependent sets of relations among persons or groups who dispose of various factors of production.

Here large-scale processes of subordination, production, and distribution attract our attention. Relevant comparisons establish similarities and differences among networks of coercion and among networks of exchange, on the one hand, and among processes of subordination, production, and distribution, on the other. At this level, general propositions will long remain risky, controversial, and extremely hard to verify. Nevertheless, without provisional assumptions concerning broad principles of variation within world systems, macrohistorical and microhistorical analyses make little sense.

With **macrohistorical** analyses, we enter the ground of history as historians ordinarily treat it. Within a given world system, we can reasonably begin to make states, regional modes of production, associations, firms, manors, armies, and a wide variety of categories, networks, and catnets our units of analysis. At this level, such large processes as proletarianization, urbanization, capital accumulation,

statemaking, and bureaucratization lend themselves to effective analyses. Comparisons, then, track down uniformities and variations
among these units, these processes, and combinations of the two.

In the shadows of world-historical and world-system analyses these
macrohistorical structures, processes, and comparisons start to look
puny indeed. Nevertheless, they are the attainable "big structures,
large processes, and huge comparisons" I actually have in mind. Their
systematic study within specific world systems—but not necessarily
throughout an entire world system—constitutes the historically
grounded treatment of structures and processes I advocate as our surest
path to knowledge.

I don't mean, however, to slight **microhistorical** knowledge. In tracing the encounters of individuals and groups with the big structures
and large processes, we make the necessary link between personal
experience and the flow of history. The structures at issue are now
relationships among persons and groups, the processes are transformations of the human interactions constituting those relationships; indeed, in microhistorical analysis the distinction between relationships
and interactions begins to lose meaning. The necessary comparisons
among relationships and their transformations are no longer huge, but
they gain coherence with attachment to relatively big structures and
large processes: the relationships between particular capitalists and particular workers reveal their pattern in the context of wider processes of
proletarianization and capital concentration.

During recent years, a kind of populist social history has grown up at
the boundaries of microhistory and macrohistory. Students of crowd
action, family structure, social mobility, revolution, urban structure,
and a number of other standard topics of social history have undertaken to study them "from the bottom up." The works of E. J. Hobs-
bawm, George Rudé, Michelle Perrot, and David Levine exemplify
the genre. One variety or another of collective biography has underlain
much of this work: the collection of uniform observations on individuals, relationships, groups, or events and their aggregation into collective portraits of the structures and processes in question.

In one perspective, such collective-biographical research takes us to
microhistory with a vengeance. Yet repeatedly populist social historians have used their evidence to answer questions about the connections between small-scale social life, on the one hand, and big struc-

tures or large processes, on the other: how the advance of capitalist property relations affected family strategies, who does what in revolutions, and so on. In evaluating the work of Wrigley and Schofield, two eminent French demographers conclude:

By its bulk and quality, the work of the Cambridge Group will, we hope, help us understand the strong links between demography (and, no doubt, all the social sciences) and history, and also understand that by dealing with frequently defective or poorly organized evidence, historical demography requires both great imagination and great rigor and can therefore attract serious researchers. [Henry and Blanchet 1983:821]

The same holds outside demography. Among other things, populist social history has had great success in challenging the sway of pernicious nineteenth-century postulates in interpretations of ordinary people's lives and actions. Microhistory thus plays an indispensable role in the analysis of big structures and large processes.

Will Total History Save Us?

At the other extreme, historians sometimes dream of a Total History sweeping all social life and its determinants into its powerful embrace. At its best, the effort to write total history has produced stunning achievements. In the hands of such masters of the genre as William McNeill and Emmanuel Le Roy Ladurie, the work sparkles with hypotheses, connections, and insights. Yet in the long run an attempt at total history will not produce a viable alternative to the understanding of big structures and large processes embodied in the nineteenth century's eight pernicious postulates.

To see why total history won't save us, let us look at one of its crowning accomplishments, Fernand Braudel's *Civilisation matérielle, économie, et capitalisme.* Two decades ago, Braudel's rambling survey of the sixteenth-century Mediterranean displayed an extraordinary sense of the interdependence among structures and changes which seemed remote from one another, or even antithetical—for instance, the rise and fall of upland banditry as a function of fluctuations in lowland state power. In *Civilisation matérielle*, he conveys that same sense at a scale that dwarfs the Mediterranean and the sixteenth century. His subject has become the experience of the entire world from the fifteenth through the eighteenth centuries. Even those four centuries do not contain him; he moves backward to the Roman Empire and forward to the 1970s. In three bulging volumes, Braudel attempts no less than a general account of the processes by which the capitalist world of the nineteenth and twentieth centuries took shape.

Braudel's account lacks the schematism of an H. G. Wells or a V. Gordon Childe. Complexities, nuances, contradictions, and doubts fill every chapter. The marvelous, abundant illustrations—plates, graphs, maps, diagrams, and tables by the hundred occupy about a fifth of the text—nearly always lend new insights, yet rarely fall neatly into a developing argument. Indeed, Braudel often makes an explicit distinction between his procedure and the assembling of evidence for a connected set of propositions. As he begins a survey of a number of instances in which agricultural capitalism became dominant, for example, he declares that "our aim is not to study these different cases for their own sakes or to seek the means of preparing an exhaustive list for the whole of Europe; we only want to sketch a line of reasoning" (Braudel 1979: II, 245). There we begin to appreciate the difficulty of the enterprise.

As crystallized in titles and subtitles, Braudel's topic falls into three divisions: (1) material culture and the structure of everyday life, (2) economy and the workings of exchange, (3) capitalism and world time. The breakdown does distinguish the emphases of his three volumes. It does not, however, reflect a causal hierarchy. It does not unfold a tight analytical model that guides the movement from one analysis to the next.

In the first part, Braudel seeks to describe how the techniques of production, distribution, and consumption varied throughout the world—especially the Western world—over the four centuries after 1400 and to show how those techniques shaped everyday experience. That first volume reveals the richness of Braudel's reading and reflection. Backed by his engaging and well-produced illustrations, he gives us disquisitions on epidemics, on agricultural techniques, on the varieties of herring, on the vagaries of clothing style. Yet a careful reader encounters surprises and disappointments. For one thing, it eventually becomes clear that—despite the ample demographic documentation on which he draws—Braudel has little concern with vital processes as such. The opening section on population avoids most of the questions on which the Wrigley-Schofield volume and other work in European historical demography have focused: the responsiveness of vital rates to economic fluctuations, the relationship between household structure and fertility, the onset of long-term declines in fertility, and so on. Braudel concerns himself with population size, growth, and decline mainly as indices of power, welfare, and vulnerability to the environment.

Again, as the volume proceeds Braudel builds up a case for inefficient transportation as a major brake on European economic growth. Yet he never quite manages to reconcile that conclusion with his earlier portrayal of the Mediterranean shipping routes as speedy "liquid roads," or with the sort of evidence Jan de Vries has assembled concerning the great importance of low-cost water transport in the economic development and communication structure of the Low Countries. At a minimum, one might have expected a comparative analysis of the advantages enjoyed by regions which had access to navigable rivers, canals, and seas.

Most of all, Braudel tantalizes his readers by raising fundamental questions, then leaving the questions to levitate themselves. One example is his discussion of Lewis Mumford's claim that nascent capitalism broke up the narrow frame of the medieval city by substituting the power of a new merchant aristocracy for that of landlords and guild-masters: "No doubt, but only to link itself to a state that conquered the cities, but only to inherit the old institutions and attitudes, and entirely incapable of doing without those institutions and attitudes" (I, 453). Another is the conclusion of a long, informative treatment of the variants and interactions of money and credit: "But if one can maintain that all is money, one can also claim, on the contrary, that all is credit: promises, reality at a distance. . . . In short, the case can be made first one way, then the other, without trickery" (I, 419). Indeed, the so-called conclusions of Braudel's entire first volume have the same ambivalent tone, with an additional note of complaint about the inadequacy of the available evidence:

I would have liked more explanations, justifications, and examples. But a book is not infinitely expansible. And in order to pin down the multiple aspects of material life, it would require close, systematic studies, not to mention whole sets of syntheses. All that is still lacking. [Braudel 1979: I, 493]

Five hundred pages into a dense compilation-cum-synthesis, one wonders. Total history apparently exceeds even Braudel's grasp.

In the second volume, Braudel proceeds from a survey of the techniques by which people in different parts of the world exchanged goods to a discussion of various types and scales of markets. He then tries to identify the peculiarities of capitalism as activity and organization, before examining its articulation with social hierarchies, structures, and broad forms of civilization. What a program!

Despite a thick, thoughtful survey of definitions, however, Braudel never quite lays out a working definition of the capitalism he has in mind. It takes a while to see that he has chosen to emphasize the conditions of exchange rather than the relations of production; he has thus aligned himself, among recent combatants on that bloody field, with Immanuel Wallerstein and André Gunder Frank and separated himself from analysts such as Robert Brenner and Witold Kula. In response to Kula's claim that the landlords who "refeudalized" eastern Europe did not, and could not, calculate as capitalists, Braudel declares:

To be sure, that is not the argument I wish to challenge. It seems to me, however, that the second serfdom was the counterpoint of a merchant capitalism which took advantage of the situation in the East, and even, to some extent, based its operation there. The great landlord was not a capitalist, but he was a tool and collaborator at the service of the capitalism of Amsterdam and other places. *He was part of the system.* [Braudel 1979: II, 235]

What, then, is that capitalist system? Gradually, Braudel reveals a vision of capitalism as an arrangement in which two or more large, coherent, market-connected "economic worlds" become linked and interdependent through the agency of big manipulators of capital. Thus, in European history, the role of **grand commerce** in the development of capitalism becomes paramount. Thus, in Braudel's view, a single capital-concentrating metropolis tends to emerge as the dominant center of any capitalist world economy.

Braudel's tack moves us in a very different direction from the identification of capitalism as a system in which the holders of capital control the basic means of production and reduce labor to a factor of production, a commodity one buys and sells; in that sort of definition, the confrontation of a capitalist with a proletarian—a person who depends for survival on the sale of labor power—occupies the very center. With Braudel, we do not recognize capitalism by its characteristic social relations, but by its general configuration. It is the difference between a blancmange and a Saint-Honoré: The smallest spoonful of the almond jelly is still blancmange, but unless crust, cream, and iced puffballs come together in the right pattern, you have no Saint-Honoré. Paradoxically, with Braudel's Saint-Honoré capitalism, once we have identified the dish as a whole, every part of it qualifies as Saint-Honoré. That is how Braudel can say of the noncapitalist landlord: He was part of the system.

The exchange-oriented definition has some analytical advantages. For one thing, it trains attention on the enormous importance of bankers, merchants, and other capitalists who knew nothing of production but plenty of prices and profits; their activities greatly facilitated changes in the relations of production. For another thing, the exchange-oriented definition brings out the continuity between small-scale and large-scale production under capitalism, and thus reduces our fixation on factories, large firms, and labor under conditions of intensive time- and work-discipline; the concentration of capital and of workspaces certainly made a difference to the autonomy of workers and the quality of work, but cottage industry and related forms of production often proceeded in a thoroughly capitalist manner. The exchange-oriented definition of capitalism steers far clear of a misleading emphasis on the technology of production.

Still, the disadvantages of Braudel's definition outweigh their advantages. The definition, in turning away from technology, abandons the relations of production entirely. Encomienda, hacienda, slavery, and, as we have seen, serfdom all become capitalist forms of labor control. Large chunks of world experience become capitalist. The historically specific analysis of the development of capitalism as a system gives way, paradoxically, to the very inquiry it was supposed to replace: the search for explanations of the British and western European "takeoff."

In fact, Braudel gives some signs of compromising the excessive broadness of his definition; in this regard, as in many others, he neglects to stick to his announced principles throughout the inquiry.

Having committed himself to a conception of capitalism involving the
linkage of two or more large, distinct markets by capital-wielding merchants, he has already committed himself to see the whole of these
markets as integral elements of a capitalist system. Yet he persists in
searching within those markets for signs of the emergence of capitalism. Thus he declares for the end of the old regime that "the
majority of the peasant world remained far from capitalism, its demands, its order, and its progress" (II, 255). Thus he concludes that
"capitalism did not invade production as such until the moment of the
Industrial Revolution, when mechanization had transformed the conditions of production in such a fashion that industry became an arena
for the expansion of profits" (II, 327). If consistency be a hobgoblin of
little minds, Braudel has no trouble escaping the demon.

When Braudel is not bedeviling us with our demands for consistency, he again parades his indecision. Throughout the second
volume of *Civilisation matérielle*, he repeatedly begins to treat the
relationship between capitalists and statemakers, then veers away.
Savor this summary of his efforts:

Finally and especially, we must leave unanswered the question which has
come up time after time: Did the state promote capitalism, or didn't it? Did it
push capitalism forward? Even if one raises doubts about the maturity of the
modern state, if—moved by recent events—one keeps one's distance from the
state, one has to concede that from the fifteenth to the eighteenth century,
the state was involved with everyone and everything, that it was one of
Europe's new forces. But does it explain everything, subject everything to its
control? No, a thousand times no. Furthermore, doesn't the reverse perspective work as well? The state favored capitalism and came to its aid—no doubt.
But let's reverse the equation: The state checks the rise of capitalism, which in
its turn can harm the state. Both things are true, successively or simultaneously, reality always being predictable and unpredictable complexity. Fa-
vorable, unfavorable, the modern state has been one of the realities amid
which capitalism has made its way, sometimes hindered, sometimes promoted, and often enough moving ahead on neutral ground. [Braudel 1979:
II, 494]

Yes, it appears, we **must** leave unanswered the question that has come
up time after time. When we arrive at the same point again and again,
we begin to suspect we are walking in circles.

The third part of Braudel's magnum opus begins with a delineation of world economies as the fundamental units of analysis and continues with a roughly chronological portrayal of the successive world economies that prevailed in Europe and elsewhere in the world. Braudel complicates his survey by simultaneous efforts to specify the changing places of smaller areas and individual cities within those world economies and—as if that were not already enough—to explain how and why Europe finally became the world's master and its prime locus of large-scale industrialization. Here especially Braudel lets shine a scintilla of sentimental chauvinism: Why did France never quite become Number One? At one moment, Braudel permits himself the speculation that the demands of Paris were to blame. In the mid-sixteenth century:

Did Paris miss the chance to acquire a measure of modernity, and France with her? That is possible. It is permissible to blame Paris' propertied classes, overly attracted to offices and land, operations which were "socially enriching, individually lucrative, and economically parasitic." [Braudel 1979: III, 280; the quotation is from Denis Richet]

Yet Braudel's gloom does not last long. Soon he sets off on a knowledgeable exploration of the changing regional divisions within the French economy—one of the finest surveys of the subject anywhere. That conversational mode provides both the charm and the frustration of the volume.

Precisely because the conversation ranges so widely, a look back over the third volume's subject matter brings astonishment: The grand themes of the first volume—population, food, clothing, technology—have almost entirely disappeared! Despite that sense of material life as a constraint on human choices so well conveyed by that first volume, we now see nothing of constraint. Braudel's discussion of the peopling of North American colonies (III, 348ff.), for example, involves no effort whatsoever to judge the contributions of changes in fertility, mortality, nuptiality, migration, or their relations to each other. Indeed, by this point Braudel has become so indifferent to population problems that he settles for graphs of English fertility and mortality changes (III, 489) borrowed from G. M. Trevelyan's ancient text on social history. Despite contrary indications in the opening volume (and despite the crucial place of Braudel's collaborators in the development of demographically based social history), Braudel makes no significant effort either to analyze demographic dynamics or to incorporate them into his explanatory system. Somehow that no longer seems to be part of the problem.

What is? Early in the second volume, Braudel calls his readers' attention to a perplexing situation. In the sixteenth century, he concludes,

the thickly settled regions of the world, subject to the pressures of large populations, seem close to one another, more or less equal. No doubt a small difference can be enough to produce first advantages, then superiority and thus, on the other side, inferiority and then subordination. Is that what happened between Europe and the rest of the world? . . . One thing looks certain to me: The gap between the West and other continents appeared *late*; to attribute it to the "rationalization" of the market economy alone, as too many of our contemporaries still have a tendency to do, is obviously simplistic.

In any case, explaining that gap, which grew more decisive with the years, is the essential problem in the history of the modern world. [Braudel 1979: II, 110-11]

The suggestion, tucked into the first volume, that a difference in energy supplies between Europe and the rest of the world might have been crucial has by this time vanished. The action of the state has, as we have seen, dissolved as a likely explanation. China, India, and other parts of the world turn out to have created commercial techniques as sophisticated as those of the Europeans. Paul Bairoch's estimates of gross national products at the end of the eighteenth century (quoted with a mixture of consternation and approval in a stop-press revision inserted at III, 460-61) show no significant advantage of western Europe over North America or China—so "initial advantage" loses its remaining shreds of credibility as an explanation.

By page 481 of the third volume, Braudel offers an indirect admission of theoretical defeat: " . . . the Industrial Revolution that overturned England, and then the whole world, was never, at any point in its path, a precisely delimited subject, a given bundle of problems, in a particular place at a certain time." All the previous history recounted in this vast review, Braudel tells us, somehow converged on that outcome. The only way to analyze industrial growth is to break it into its many elements, to take up those elements one by one, and to trace their multiple connections. That Braudel's earlier analyses forecast just such an intellectual strategy and that Braudel follows the strategy with subtle brilliance do not eliminate a certain disappointment at Braudel's surrender.

Near the start of the third volume, it looks as though Braudel will try to perform his explanatory miracle by relying on Immanuel Wallerstein's model of the European world system, especially its distinction of core, semi-periphery, and periphery. But Braudel eventually opts for a more relaxed identification of the world's economically dependent regions, leans against Wallerstein's claim that the European capitalist world economy was the first one not to consolidate into a political empire, doubts that empires as such stifle the potential of world economies, and maps out multiple European world economies well before the supposedly critical unification of the sixteenth century.

Braudel follows Wallerstein especially in building his account around the successive hegemonies of capitalist metropolises: Venice, Genoa, Antwerp, Amsterdam, London, New York. He accepts, for a while, Wallerstein's unconventional characterization of the seventeenth-century Dutch and English states as "strong" states, on the ground that their modest apparatus demonstrated the efficiency with which their dominant classes could work their will. When self-conscious about the problem, he remains faithful to Wallerstein's focus on conditions of exchange, rather than relations of production, as the essential features of capitalism. But in fact he neither uses the core/semi-periphery/periphery scheme as a tool of analysis nor attempts to test it by means of his vast store of information. It is a grand story, elegantly told—and nothing like a definitive solution to the "essential problem."

Should we have expected anything else from a man of Braudel's intellectual temper? He approaches a problem by enumerating its elements; fondling its ironies, contradictions, and complexities; confronting the various theories scholars have proposed; and giving each theory its historical due. The sum of all theories is, alas, no theory. We end our long journey delighted with all we have seen, grateful for our guide's wisdom and perspicacity, inspired to revisit some of the hidden corners he has revealed, but no more than dimly aware of the master plan.

If Braudel could not bring off the coup, who could? Perhaps someone else will succeed in writing a "total history" that accounts for the entire development of capitalism and the full growth of the European state system. At least for the time being, we are better off treating Braudel's giant essay as a source of inspiration rather than a model of analysis. Except with a Braudel lending it extra power, a vessel so large and complex seems destined to sink before it reaches the far shore.

The Case For Huge (But Not Stupendous) Comparisons

From this point on, I will neglect world-historical, world-systemic, and microhistorical structures, processes, and comparisons. Macrohistory—the study of big structures and large processes within particular world systems—will dominate the rest of this book. When our nineteenth-century forebears thought they were discovering universal laws of social process, they were usually reasoning within the confines of the capitalist world system they knew; in order to improve on their work, we must be aware of other levels of analysis, but pursue structures and processes at the same level as they. Furthermore, we are at the moment much better prepared to make advances in macrohistorical and microhistorical analysis than to sweep across world-historical and world-systemic space.

Finally, since my own studies generally proceed at the edges of microhistorical and macrohistorical analysis, and since I believe passionately in the value of getting the microhistory right in order to understand the macrohistory, it is easier for me to illustrate the value of different comparative approaches to structures and processes at the macrohistorical level. My apologies to those who think smaller, or much larger.

Our task, then, is to fix accounts of specific structures and processes within particular world systems to historically grounded generalizations concerning those world systems. Let us shrink the scope somewhat and concentrate on western Europe since 1500. For that block of time and space, possible organizing statements concerning national states include:

1 Relatively independent political units lacking extensive centrally *nation-state.* controlled armed force, major geographic barriers to conquest, or a stand-off of adjacent powers generally lost their autonomy and were absorbed into larger national states.
2 War-making tended to expand the national fiscal apparatus. For *war-making capacity.* those that succeeded, war-making and preparations for war created the major structures of the national state.
3 Large reductions in the total number of autonomous European states, realignments of boundaries, and alterations of the relations *consolidation.* among states occurred at the ends of major wars.
4 Great rebellions occurred chiefly either when rulers sought major *rebellions* increases in the contributions of their subject populations for war or when war and its aftermath weakened the repressive capacity of rulers.

Historically grounded statements we might hazard for the development of capitalism include:

5 Before the nineteenth-century implosion of capital and labor, pro-*pre-19th c. capital/labor concentration* letarianization of the population took place mainly in the country-side and occurred at least as widely in agriculture as in industry.
6 Nevertheless, petty capitalists organized manufacturing in house-holds and small shops through much of the European countryside *deind. strategy* during the seventeenth and eighteenth centuries; in a sense, great rural regions **de**industrialized during the nineteenth-century implosion of capital and labor.
7 On the whole, that implosion **reduced**, rather than increasing, the residential mobility of the western European population. How-*movement of population* ever, the distance and permanence of the average move increased significantly in the same process, and temporary flows of relatively unskilled workers—largely from Europe's low-income peripheries——greatly accelerated.
8 Until the nineteenth century, few capitalists knew how to manu-facture anything; in general, workers held the secrets of produc-*knowledge of manufacture* tion, while capitalists specialized in buying and selling workers' products. By the end of the nineteenth century, few workers knew how to make the entire item they helped manufacture, and capi-talists thereby held the secrets of production.

These statements are not postulates. They stand subject to refinement and falsification. Some or all of them may well be false as stated. But until revised or replaced, they will serve as frames for more specific analyses of structural change.

How? Take generalization 8 as an example. If we may take for granted—however provisionally—that during the nineteenth century many capitalists and workers were struggling for control of decisions concerning what to produce and how, we can examine the conditions under which employees were more or less successful in that struggle, in confidence that we are helping to explain a major transformation in the organization of production. If we discover (as well we might) that a capitalist's ability to control access to energy sources and raw materials facilitating mass production—coal rather than wood, cotton rather than flax, for instance—fostered a more rapid capitalist victory in the struggle for control of production, then we would have a warrant to investigate whether the shift away from widely available energy sources and raw materials (1) gave capitalists the means to concentrate capital as never before, (2) became a deliberate strategy of capitalists who sought to reorganize the whole productive process, (3) administered the coup de grâce to small-scale production with extensive workers' control.

One could arrive at such conclusions without arguing for a moment that in all places and times the narrowing of energy sources and raw materials for production results in industrial capitalism or employer's hegemony within the workplace. Indeed, where property rights in energy sources or raw materials are difficult to secure—which is the case in many noncapitalist modes of production—an employer's shift toward narrowly available energy sources and raw materials could well be self-defeating. Thus a generalization may hold very widely within its own historical domain, yet be quite contingent.

No Safety in Numbers

As we move toward the identification of historically specific regularities in social structures and processes, we should also move away from the habit of packing large numbers of cases into extensive statistical analyses. On the whole, comparative studies of big structures and large processes yield more intellectual return when investigators examine relatively small numbers of instances. That is not because of the intrinsically greater value of small numbers, but because large numbers give an illusory sense of security.

With small numbers, the student of a structure or process has little choice but to pay attention to the historical circumstances and particular characteristics of the cases at hand and thus to work harder at meeting the commonsense conditions for effective comparison. With large numbers, critical defenses and familiarity with context decline. Little of long-term value to the social sciences has emerged from the hundreds of studies conducted during the last few decades that have run statistical analyses including most of the world's national states.

The chief exceptions have been statistical descriptions in the style of Paul Bairoch and theoretically motivated investigations coupled with case studies in the style of Jeffery Paige. Yet during the same period most of the outstanding, influential studies of large-scale structural change have been explicitly, self-consciously comparative. The lesson reads: Stick with careful comparisons of small numbers until you have a very clear idea what you need from large numbers and how to make the comparisons valid.

Anyone who surveys recent big studies of large-scale structural change employing small numbers of cases notices the remarkable staying power of the classics. In one form or another, Durkheim, Tocqueville, Weber, and, especially, Marx continue to set the problems— even for those investigators who intend to leave the grandfathers behind. Tocqueville and Weber peep over Theda Skocpol's shoulder as she herself invokes Marx. Reinhard Bendix echoes Weber. So does S. N. Eisenstadt, while making an occasional bow to Tocqueville and Durkheim. Perry Anderson's *Lineages of the Absolutist State* undertakes self-consciously to fill out Marx's account of the state. Immanuel Wallerstein incorporates a controversial version of Marx's account of capitalism into his own model of the capitalist world system. And Barrington Moore, as we shall see, draws heavily on Marxist thought without adopting its full structure.

None of these scholars accepts the classic statements supinely. All of them realize that no one—not even the greats—has yet solved the problems they are addressing. That is why the problems deserve atten-

tion. But latter-day students of big structures and large processes generally find that more recent theorizing, for all its utility in the details,
does not match the forceful setting of problems they find in the classic
comparative essays. The revival of Marxist thought has grown in part
from the critique of theories of modernization and development, but it
has also resulted from a two-step process: First scholars turn away from
studies of big structures and large processes that concentrate on the
present and decide to take history seriously. Then they discover the
great theoretical resources of Marxist thought for historical research.

Marxists have, on the average, moved to meet the newcomers.
Being relatively satisfied with their ability to analyze the organization
of production, Marxists have become concerned about the weakness of
their analyses of the organization of coercion. From Marx onward,
coercion has always figured in Marxist analyses of structural change.
Marxist treatments of feudalism, for example, call attention to the
dependence of that mode of production on noneconomic coercion of
peasants. Marx considered capitalism to be unique in its exclusive
reliance on economic constraints: The genius of the system, in Marx's
account, was to make submission to exploitation serve the worker's
short-run interest at the expense of long-term loss.

Even under capitalism, however, changes in the organization of
production and increases in the level of exploitation commonly involved coercion; *Capital* dwells on the forcible dispossession of peasants and artisans. Subsequent Marxist analyses, furthermore, have
stressed the coercion employers used in tightening work-discipline,
speeding up production, and reducing the autonomy of skilled
workers.

Nevertheless, the organization of coercion in general has had an
uncertain place in Marxist analysis. Does it have its own logic, parallel
to that of the organization of production, or does it ultimately reduce
to the logic of production? Nowhere is the uncertainty more trou-
blesome than in the analysis of governments, and especially of states:
To what extent, how, and when, do states act independently of the
organization of production?

Recent Marxist, neo-Marxist, quasi-Marxist, and crypto-Marxist
writers have worried and fought over that question more than any
other. Theda Skocpol broke with Barrington Moore and with standard

Marxist arguments on precisely that question; at all levels, including the level of the state, she saw the organization of coercion as having an independent logic and influence, not entirely reducible to the logic of production. Perry Anderson's tour de force was to save most of the determination of state structure by the organization of production. He did so by arguing that, despite appearances, the Absolutist state grew up as an instrument of the feudal nobility. In his view, the difference in state structure between the eastern and western halves of Europe resulted from the divergent interests of their landed classes.

Both the turn away from developmental theories and the renaissance of Marxist thought have promoted a revival of genuinely historical work in the social sciences. By "genuinely historical," I mean studies assuming that the time and place in which a structure or process appears make a difference to its character, that the sequence in which similar events occur has a substantial impact on their outcomes, and that the existing record of past structures and processes is problematic, requiring systematic investigation in its own right instead of lending itself immediately to social-scientific syntheses.

Thus we find Douglas Hibbs beginning his career with a vast, atheoretical, ahistorical, cross-national statistical analysis of the "determinants" of political violence, then moving rapidly to careful long-term comparisons of struggles for control of national income in European countries. Thus we find Bertrand Badie and Pierre Birnbaum building a sociology of the state around a careful historical analysis of the development of different forms of state in Europe and America. Thus we find Victoria Bonnell, a sociologist, plunging deep into Russian sources to emerge with close comparisons between the working classes of St. Petersburg and Moscow, on the one hand, and between working-class organization in Russia and western Europe, on the other. As compared with conventional wisdom concerning prerevolutionary Russia, Bonnell's analysis of the period 1905–1914 reveals surprising activism on the part of skilled workers, extensive worker organization in periods of lowered repression, and supple adaptation of Bolshevik programs to workers' own articulated objectives. There it is: Sociologists, anthropologists, political scientists, and an occasional economist have begun to work at getting the history right before generalizing, in order to be able to generalize soundly.

Ways of Seeing

All pernicious postulates discarded, suppose we still want to under-stand how our world got into its present sorry state and what alterna-tives to it might exist. How can we compare big structures and large processes for these purposes?

We must make sure that the classical logic of comparison, which guides a search for concomitant variation, fits our aims like a sweat-shirt and not like a straitjacket; it should make the exercise more effective, rather than making it impossible. No one should take the rules to require a search for the perfect pair of structures or processes: exquisitely matched on every variable except the purported cause and the supposed effect. Nor should anyone take them to require the pursuit of final causes; we should be delighted to discover the proxi-mate causes of social phenomena. Nor do the rules forbid us to seek principles of covariation beginning "In so far as. . . ." Nor, finally, do they demand **complete** explanations—explanations leaving no ounce of variance unaccounted for. The rules enjoin us to examine apparent covariation with high seriousness and to eliminate spurious causes with great ruthlessness.

In order to do so, we must be sure of the units we are comparing. Just so long as we remain clear and consistent, we have our choice of a great variety of populations, categories, networks, and catnets: firms, regions, social classes, kin groups, churches, trading nets, interna-tional alliances, and many, many others. The trick is to have criteria for identifying real populations, categories, networks, or catnets as specimens of the sort of unit about which we are theorizing.

If we abandon societies as units of analysis, then, we need not abandon national states. We need only be cautious: remember that the area and population controlled by that state, and not some mystical entity existing independently of the state, delimit the analysis; change the boundaries of the observation as the state's own boundaries change; recognize the interdependence of adjacent states. But we have many other choices than states: international power blocs, regions marked out by hierarchies of cities or markets, regional modes of production, social classes, linguistic groups, and so on.

The choice among many possible units of analysis lays the theoretical responsibility directly where it belongs: on the theorist. No theorist can responsibly retreat to vague statements about "society" when she has a clear choice among statements about national states, international power blocs, regions, regional modes of production, social classes, linguistic groups, and many other social units. Only when theorists of big structures specify to which units their statements apply can we hope to organize the evidence efficiently and to determine how well their statements hold up to theoretical scrutiny.

Let us distinguish among several different ways of comparing big structures and large processes. To be more precise, let us classify the different sorts of **propositions** at which we might reasonably aim a comparative analysis. In a standard sociological simplification, let us define and then combine two dimensions of comparison: **share of all instances** and **multiplicity of forms. In share**, the statement resulting from a comparison can range from a single instance (getting the characteristics of the case at hand right) to all instances of the phenomenon (getting the characteristics of all cases right).

In **multiplicity**, the statement emerging from a comparison can range from single (all instances of a phenomenon have common properties) to multiple (many forms of the phenomenon exist). Cross-classifying the two dimensions of variation yields a familiar sort of diagram:

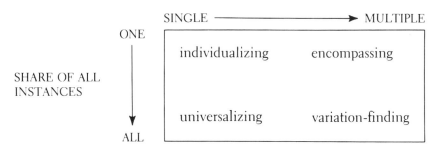

MULTIPLICITY OF FORMS

	SINGLE ⟶ MULTIPLE	
ONE	individualizing	encompassing
SHARE OF ALL INSTANCES		
ALL	universalizing	variation-finding

Thus a purely individualizing comparison treats each case as unique, taking up one instance at a time, and minimizing its common properties with other instances. A pure universalizing comparison, on the other hand, identifies common properties among all instances of a phenomenon. We have a choice, then, among individualizing, universalizing, variation-finding, and encompassing comparisons of big structures and large processes.

We should be clear about what this classification classifies. It does **not** depend on the strict internal logic of the comparison: whether all characteristics of the cases at hand except two are supposed to be the same, whether the social structures or processes being compared belong to the same order, and so on. Nor does it depend on the nature of those structures and processes: large-scale or small-scale, simple or complex, dynamic or static, and so forth. It depends instead on the relationship between observation and theory. Comparisons are general to the extent that their users are attempting to make all cases in a category conform to the same principle. Comparisons are multiple to the extent that their users are trying to establish that the cases in a category take multiple forms. Thus the classification classifies strategies, not tactics, of comparison.

First comes the **individualizing** comparison, in which the point is to contrast specific instances of a given phenomenon as a means of grasping the peculiarities of each case. Thus Reinhard Bendix contrasts changes in British and German political life with a view to clarifying how British workers acquired relatively full participation in national politics, while German workers kept finding themselves excluded.

At the general end of the same side we have the **universalizing** comparison. It aims to establish that every instance of a phenomenon follows essentially the same rule. Take, for example, the recurrent effort to construct a natural history of economic growth, either through the specification of necessary and sufficient conditions for takeoff or through the identification of the stages through which every industrializing country must pass, once begun.

On the other side from the individualizing and the universalizing comparison we find the **variation-finding** comparison. It is supposed to establish a principle of variation in the character or intensity of a phenomenon by examining systematic differences among instances. Jeffery Paige's *Agrarian Revolution* qualifies as variation-finding by virtue of its proposal to link different sorts of rural political action to varying combinations of workers' source of income, ruling class's source of income, and governmental repressiveness.

The fourth and final use of comparison is neither individualizing, universalizing, nor variation-finding, but **encompassing**. It places different instances at various locations within the same system, on the way to explaining their characteristics as a function of their varying relationships to the system as a whole. In recent years, Immanuel Wallerstein's brand of world-system analysis, with its placement of world regions in the core, semi-periphery, or periphery of a single capitalist world system, has provided an influential model of encompassing comparison.

All four strategies work for some purposes. The Tillys' *Rebellious Century*, for instance, relies mainly on individualizing comparison, although occasionally it gestures toward universalizing and variation-finding. In that book, Louise Tilly, Richard Tilly, and I look chiefly at the ways in which popular collective action (especially as represented by strikes and collective violence) fluctuated and changed as a function of statemaking and the development of capitalism in Italy, France, and Germany from roughly 1830 to 1930. Comparisons among Italy, France, and Germany serve chiefly to bring out the distinctive features of the three experiences; they individualize. Nevertheless, from time to time we use them to search for invariant common properties of collective action (and thus to universalize), or to explore possible principles of variation implicit in the collective-action consequences of the rather different ways the German, Italian, and French states came into being (and thus to engage in variation-finding).

Immanuel Wallerstein's *Modern World System*, in contrast, alternates between individualizing and encompassing comparison. On the one hand, Wallerstein strives to get the characteristics of the capitalist world system right by means of contrasts with earlier empires, with China, and with Europe itself before about 1500; those comparisons individualize. On the other, he puts much of his effort into arguing that the experiences of particular regions within the capitalist world system (which he tends to identify with particular states such as Spain and England) depended on the niches they occupied with respect to the system as a whole—especially whether they lay in the core, periphery, or semi-periphery. That effort encompasses.

The chapters to come will discuss the work of Reinhard Bendix (largely individualizing), Theda Skocpol (often universalizing), Barrington Moore, Jr. (frequently variation-finding), and Stein Rokkan

(usually encompassing). For the moment, we can lay out the central
comparative practices of Paige, Wallerstein, the Tillys, Bendix, Skocpol, Moore, and Rokkan in this scheme:

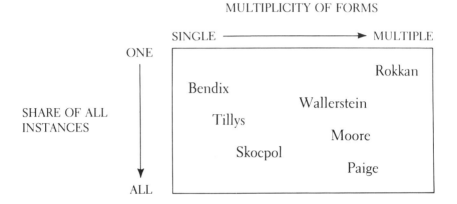

MULTIPLICITY OF FORMS

SINGLE ──────────────→ MULTIPLE

ONE

SHARE OF ALL
INSTANCES

ALL

Bendix

Rokkan

Wallerstein

Tillys

Moore

Skocpol

Paige

Looking at Comparisons

Arthur Stinchcombe's daringly comparative *Economic Sociology* takes
the contemporary Karimojong population of East Africa, eighteenth-
century France, and the twentieth-century United States as its three
principal instances. Although Stinchcombe indulges in a good deal of
individualizing and a bit of universalizing, he uses his comparisons
mainly for the purpose of finding variation. Starting that book, Stinchcombe complains that "comparative sociologists are a vanishing
breed," although he counts himself among the breed (Stinchcombe
1983: vii).

Surely Stinchcombe is wrong. In America alone, Barrington
Moore, Theda Skocpol, Michael Hechter, Gerhard Lenski, Reinhard
Bendix, and many others continue to work with telling comparisons.
As Raymond Grew has remarked, the comparison of historical processes "is especially congenial to economics, sociology, and some
schools of anthropology." "Many of the most often-cited works of
recent historical comparison," continues Grew, "belong in this category, although significantly enough, most have not been written by
scholars professionally trained as historians" (Grew 1980: 764–65). In

this connection, Grew mentions, among others, the work of S. N. Eisenstadt, Samuel P. Huntington, Barrington Moore, and Immanuel Wallerstein.

How could so shrewd an observer as Stinchcombe relegate all of these outstanding scholars—and himself—to a vanishing breed? The trouble, I think, lies here: Stinchcombe, a consummate hunter for principles of variation, hesitates to recognize the other forms of comparison as genuine comparison. Although I share his preference for variation-finding comparisons—where they are feasible and appropriate—in the chapters to come I hope to show that individualizing, universalizing, and, especially, encompassing comparisons also have legitimate, significant parts to play in building our understanding of big social structures and large social processes.

Raymond Grew also points out that "the comparison of historical processes also evokes resistance, even suspicion, among many historians" (Grew 1980: 765). There I have a message for historians. They have great advantages in the building of effective comparisons. They should not abandon those advantages to political scientists, sociologists, and other social scientists. If the evils they reject are the search for universal historical laws and the forcing of historical experience into ahistorical categories, the remedy to the evils is not the abandonment of deliberate comparison, but its rooting in genuine historical structures and processes. The following chapters will, I hope, show that historical understanding has much to gain from the construction of historically grounded, comparative social science.

Concentrating on European experience since 1500, let us ask what strategies of comparison help make that experience intelligible. If the inquiry yields interesting answers, those answers will naturally lead to their conversion into questions for the next inquiry.

The chapters to come take up in turn the individualizing, universalizing, variation-finding, and encompassing strategies for comparing big structures and large processes. The major examples in each chapter—specific works of Reinhard Bendix, Theda Skocpol, Barrington Moore, Jr., and Stein Rokkan—all present first-rate comparative analyses of big structures and large processes. My aim is not to summarize or assess the complete work of any of these scholars, or even to offer full evaluations of the works I do discuss; it is to show strategies of comparison in action.

For the most part, Bendix, Skocpol, Moore, and Rokkan reject the pernicious ninteenth-century postulates and seek to build their arguments on strong historical evidence. Better than any exhortation, then, they illustrate the alternative to ahistorical analyses assuming the existence of societies, of differentiation as the master process, and so on. They display the value of tearing large-scale comparison away from the abstract, ahistorical stake to which social scientists have often chained it and of attaching it instead to historically specific experiences of change.

5

INDIVIDUALIZING COMPARISONS

The Will to Individualize

Comparing large social units in order to identify their singularities has been with us a long time. When Montesquieu compared different parts of the world with respect to climate, topography, social life, and politics, he sometimes appeared to be seeking principles of variation, but generally ended up with singularities. He was attempting, after all, to show that environment shaped character, that forms of government corresponded strongly to the character of the people in their social settings, that each form of government called for its own variety of law, and that lack of correspondence among national character, governmental form, and law tended to undermine governmental authority. Such a theory of correspondences leads naturally to individualizing comparisons. When discussing corruption, for example, Montesquieu follows "the logic inherent in a method that refuses to draw conclusions applicable to all distinctive types of states. Rather he deduces his generalizations from the specific structure and ruling passion of each type" (Richter 1977: 82).

To the delight of Albert Hirschman, Montesquieu follows precisely that principle in Part Four of the *Esprit des lois*. There, speaking of

England without quite saying so, Montesquieu declares that "it is fortunate for men to be in a situation in which, though their passions may prompt them to be wicked (*méchants*), they have nevertheless an interest in not being so." "Here," exults Hirschman, "is a truly magnificent generalization built on the expectation that the interests—that is, commerce and its corollaries, such as the bill of exchange—would inhibit the passions and the passion-induced "wicked" actions of the powerful" (Hirschman 1977: 73). The irony is that Montesquieu formulates his principle, which so easily becomes a principle of variation in the hands of such a theorist as Hirschman, not to account for general patterns of variation among states, but to single out and understand the peculiarities of seafaring commercial states.

Let no one mistake my point, Individualizing comparisons build on the strengths of historically grounded social science. One of the greatest contributions social scientists can make is to establish exactly what is particular about a particular historical experience—including our own contemporary experience. The discovery that today's poor countries were **not** recapitulating the economic-growth experiences of Britain, France, or the United States contributed powerfully to our understanding of contemporary social change; that discovery resulted largely from individualizing comparisons. As a frequent practitioner of individualizing comparison, I have no desire to run it down. The point, then, is not that individualizing comparison is a bungled attempt at generalization, but that it differs significantly from universalizing, encompassing, and variation-finding comparison.

If we needed a pedigree for individualizing comparison, its use by Max Weber would suffice. When Weber started elaborating his great taxonomies, he bowed toward generalization. When he spoke of rationalization and charisma, he gestured toward universalizing comparison. But his wide comparisons of religious systems served mainly to specify the uniqueness of the achieving, accumulating, rationalizing, bureaucratizing West. To a large degree, Max Weber used comparisons for the purpose of individualizing.

To be sure, "the West" is a very big individual. Still, the point of Weber's analysis is less to find the common properties of many instances or to identify a principle of variation than to get the West right. As Reinhard Bendix says,

His sociology of religion culminates in the attempt to explain the initial differentiation between mystic contemplation and ascetic activism. In one sense the study was complete once he had explained the origin of ethical rationalism by the contribution of ancient Jewish prophecy. Yet in another sense all of Weber's essays in the sociology of religion are a mere preface to what he had not yet explained for the West. [Bendix 1960: 284–85]

Weber, continues Bendix, never abandoned the search for the secret of rationalism's triumph in the West. The individualizing comparison dominated all the rest.

In our own day, Reinhard Bendix has himself been one of the great practitioners of individualizing comparison. Faithful to the examples of Max Weber and Otto Hintze, he has sought the features distinguishing the few relatively successful cases of durable parliamentary government from all other historical experiences. He has done so with theoretical parsimony, and with exceptional clarity concerning what has to be explained. Arthur Stinchcombe tells a pleasant tale:

In my first year of graduate-school, I turned in a paper to Reinhard Bendix called "Rhetorical Opportunities in Some Theories of Social Change." After some discussion of the substance of the paper, he made a comment that has shaped my attitude toward "theory." He said, "You know, a little bit of theory goes a long way." He went on to say I ought to decide what phenomena I wanted to explain. [Stinchcombe 1968: v]

Bendix has heeded his own teaching. In *Work and Authority in Industry*, he uses a comparison among Russia, England, East Germany, and the United States to determine the conditions under which entrepreneurs acquired room for maneuver. Its overall intellectual purpose, comments Arthur Stinchcombe, "is to explore the historical sources of a 'pluralist' rather than a 'totalitarian' resolution of the problems of labor relations" (Stinchcombe 1978: 104). We see at once why the two pairs of comparisons, Russia/England and Germany/United States, come into play.

In the long run, Bendix aims at principles explaining all the various experiences he analyzes. Furthermore, Bendix's conclusion that industrializing everywhere brings bureaucratization of the workplace has a universalizing air, while his conclusion that confidence in the good faith of subordinates was crucial to entrepreneurial flexibility begins to sound like variation-finding. But the bulk of his comparative effort actually treats Russia or Germany as a reversing mirror in which to examine Anglo-American traits more carefully. Bendix makes no effort to discover, for example, the general conditions affecting confidence in the good faith of subordinates. His explanations, in the last analysis, come down to the persistence of old authority patterns into the age of concentrated industry. That is individualizing comparison par excellence.

If Bendix concentrates on the singularities of Russia, England, Germany, or the United States, he does not content himself with simple description, with mere narrative. He seeks to find the recurrent patterns within each national experience. In one of his many reflective general essays on method, Bendix declares that "where analysis emphasizes the chronology and individual sequence of such solutions, it belongs to the historian; where it emphasizes the pattern of these solutions, it belongs to the sociologist" (Bendix 1963: 537).

I object to that division of labor. As I see it, good historical analysts (whether they call themselves sociologists or historians) use the reconstruction of chronology and individual sequence as a means of identifying recurrent patterns and of verifying their existence. Nevertheless, the pattern-finding role Bendix assigns to sociologists applies to the study of single nations taken singly; comparison with other national experiences serves mainly to bring out the special features of the national pattern.

The same individualizing ambition dominates Bendix's *Nation-Building and Citizenship*. In that work, he offers comparisons of Western Europe, Russia, Japan, Germany, and India—most often pair by pair. The book aims to specify the conditions for creation of a national political community: a national state in which citizens have enough confidence in their rulers and their institutions that the rulers can handle change without utterly destroying their capacity to rule. Bendix deliberately cites Max Weber, Fustel de Coulanges, and Hannah Arendt as predecessors along the same path. "In these and similar studies," he writes,

a recurrent issue of the human condition is identified in order to examine empirically how men in different societies have encountered that issue. If the emphasis is to be on *men acting* in societies, these studies will have to give full weight not only to the *conditioning* of these actions but in principle also to the fact that men have *acted* in the face of the agonizing dilemmas that confront them. To maintain this balanced approach, comparative studies should not only highlight the contrasts existing between different human situations and social structures, but also underscore the inescapable artificiality of conceptual distinctions and the consequent need to move back and forth between the empirical evidence and the benchmark concepts which Max Weber called "ideal types." In this way such studies reveal the network of interrelations which distinguishes one social structure from another. [Bendix 1977: 22; emphases in text]

The business at hand, then, is the distinction of one social structure from another.

Kings or People?

Bendix's *Kings or People* greatly widens the stage, but does not alter the basic script. On a world scale, *Kings or People* examines two alternative bases of government—hereditary monarchy and popular sovereignty—and asks how the second succeeded the first in western Europe from the sixteenth century onward.

Max Weber casts a long shadow over the book. Weber's influence appears not only in the fundamental statement of the problem, but also in Bendix's insistence on legitimacy as the basis of rule; in his basing of legitimacy on systems of belief; in his recurrence to Christianity, Buddhism, Confucianism, and Islam when explaining differences among the political systems of western Europe, Japan, China, and the Muslim world; and in his relatively slight concern about the technical problems of taxation, warfare, repression, budgets, reconciliation of competing interests and other essential activities of governments. Although Bendix does sustain comparisons across the world's empires, furthermore, he organizes those comparisons so as to close in on the peculiarities that permitted western Europe to host the transition from rule in the name of the king to rule in the name of the people. His comparisons individualize.

For the Bendix of *Kings or People*, a little theory still goes a long way. To the slim theoretical tool kit of his previous books, this Bendix adds only one major device: a demonstration effect in which the people of one state strive to create the political arrangements they see in another state. He couples the demonstration effect with the theory of ideological continuity that he used repeatedly in his earlier works. More or less self-consciously, Bendix adopts the new device in order to escape the effects of seeing internal differentiation—more precisely, the internal differentiation associated with industrialization—as the driving force of change. By itself, that internal differentiation would produce similar changes and outcomes in a wide variety of countries and thereby contradict the premise from which Bendix began.

In principle, such a theory of diffusion opens the way to a move from individualizing comparison toward variation-finding. Following Alex Inkeles, for example, Bendix could treat the extent and rapidity of diffusion of political models in one country or another as a function of the involvement of ordinary people in factories, markets, and other settings exposing them to those models: the more rapid and massive the creation of those settings, the quicker the diffusion. But Bendix characteristically clings to individuality. "In order to preserve a sense of historical particularity while comparing different countries," he writes, "I ask the same or at least similar questions of very different contexts and thus allow for divergent answers" (Bendix 1978: 15).

In fact, Bendix goes beyond a mere methodological mandate; he mistrusts standardizing schemes and finds diversity everywhere. Here is a crucial summary:

England, France, Germany, Japan, Russia, and China have participated in a worldwide movement of nationalism and of government by popular mandate, though each country has done so in its own way. My account attempts to show that nationalism has become a universal condition in our world because the sense of backwardness in one's own country has led to ever new encounters with the "advanced model" or development of another country. I wish to show that the problems faced by each modernizing country were largely unique. Even the countries which had been building their political institutions for centuries had to cope with unprecedented problems in the process of modernization. Today, new states looking for analogues or precedents in other countries have more models to choose from than ever before, but their histories and the earlier development of other countries have hardly prepared them for the tasks of state-building. [Bendix 1978: 5]

Three assumptions suffuse Bendix's argument: **first,** that despite the demonstration effect each state works out its fate in considerable independence of all the rest; **second,** that within each state previous institutional history and contemporary beliefs place enormous constraints on the possible solutions to recognized problems; **third,** that the pivotal events are not alterations in the structure of production or of power, but changes in prevailing ideas, beliefs, and justifications. Through their stress on the causal influence of conditions that are unique to each state, the three assumptions push the whole analysis back toward individualization.

Bendix builds his analysis as a series of narratives punctuated by summaries and comparisons. In the book's first half, he presents the ways that kings established, justified, and defended their rule; quick observations on Germanic, Islamic, and Chinese experiences provide the background for extended treatments of Japan, Russia, Imperial Germany/Prussia, and England, followed by a general discussion of kingly authority. In the second half, Bendix traces the emergence of rule in the name of the people; the histories of England, France, Germany, Japan, and Russia do the bulk of the work and lead to a final review of the twentieth-century situation. In neither half does he worry much about explaining the actions of ordinary people; throughout the book, the problem is to explain the actions of rulers and of claimants to rule.

Indeed, Bendix adopts a problematic, if conventional, account of European popular mobilization: in that account, the growth of cities and the commercialization of land, labor, and capital promoted the appearance of educated minorities. Then: "Various groups of educated minorities became alerted to the social and cultural position of their own society in relation to the 'demonstration of advances' beyond their frontiers, a process which acquired momentum in Europe in the sixteenth century and has since spread to most other countries of the world" (Bendix 1978: 258). Ordinary people disappear from Bendix's history, except as a breeding ground for new elites and as a field in which those new elites sow their implicitly revolutionary ideas. Neither the great European popular rebellions nor the long, hard bargaining of royal and ecclesiastical officials with peasants, artisans, and proletarians over taxation, the tithe, military service, and church control of family life have any place in the argument. Those are, I think, serious omissions.

As Bendix works out this analysis in detail for England, the major changes of his sixteenth century include the price revolution and the Reformation of Henry VIII. But they do not include the proletarianization of the rural population or the proliferation of trading networks tended by small capitalists. The century's great popular rebellions dissolve into a single sentence: "Great anxiety was caused by the widespread distress due to enclosures, by vagrancy in the countryside, and by sporadic rebellions" (Bendix 1978: 282). Consistent with his emphasis on beliefs and elites, Bendix centers his portrait of the English sixteenth century on the rise of Puritanism. There he sees a strong parallel between the development of the new religious creed and the rise of parliamentary government. Both, thinks Bendix, rested on the paradox of equality within a well-defined elite: The equality of all believers before God separated them sharply from nonbelievers, just as the equality of parliamentarians before the king placed a gulf between them and common people.

Similarly, in studying France of the seventeenth and eighteenth centuries, Bendix has nothing to say of the country's vast seventeenth-century rebellions, of the energetic growth of small-scale industry, of the capitalization of agriculture, of the royal struggle with popular Protestantism, of the broad resistance to royal taxation and seigneurial aggrandizement. Bendix's account deals with governmental structure, with French reactions to England and America, with the development of a critical spirit among writers, parlementary officials, and Free-masons.

Cracks in the Foundation

When Bendix comes to Germany, the lack of any strong analogy to the Puritans or the Philosophes causes him trouble. The eighteenth century and the beginning of the nineteenth work well enough. The attention of German princes and courts to French models looks like a demonstration effect, while the creativity of Lessing, Schiller, Goethe,

Kant, Fichte, and Hegel resembles the formation of an intellectual counter-elite. But given that start, the later nineteenth century did not produce the appropriate drive for democratization.

Bendix does not consider socialists and organized workers to have constituted a serious opposition. His preferred candidates, civil servants, remain loyal longer than the general argument makes convenient: "The question was how long these officials would maintain their liberal outlook in economic affairs without being won over by the agitation for popular representation which spread in part through the public implementation of that liberal outlook" (Bendix 1978: 426). The Prussian revolution of 1848, lacking a broad intellectual movement, and ending with a constitution of liberal sentiments and authoritarian institutions, comes on as an anomaly.

Bendix finally reasons that the poor fit between his scheme and Germany's experience helps explain Germany's twentieth-century wanderings:

Nevertheless, the idea of a bill of rights and of popular sovereignty had been at least verbally embraced, and the question was how long the people would remain under the political tutelage of the monarch and his court party. We know today that Germany was unprepared for the advent of popular sovereignty when that tutelage was destroyed in 1918. The history of the Weimar Republic demonstrated that the mentality of hometownsmen, a legal order primarily upheld by officials, and the idealization of Bildung and duty had provided a weak foundation for national citizenship. Few people had internalized the "rules of the game" of democratic politics and without that internalization a mandate of the people cannot function. [Bendix 1978: 430]

Despite this bold bid to save the argument, the passage's tone reveals some perplexity. Bendix is apparently aware that the German experience shakes his general scheme: no strong demonstration effect, no new elite converting that demonstration into a usable ideology, no easy translation of a democratic ideology into popular opposition to hereditary monarchy. Here, more than almost anywhere else in the book, we sense the trouble caused by ignoring ordinary people.

Let me be clear about it: These emphases and omissions follow directly from the analytical program Bendix adopts. They are deliberate. Bendix uses his cases and comparisons to argue the importance of variation in the past availability of systems of belief as a cause of present variation in forms of government. What is more, the very fidelity of his use of individualizing comparison leads him to identify the difficulties in the German case. My complaint comes to this: There is no way to specify the impact of those systems of belief without examining the organization and action of the people who are supposed to be mobilizing around the beliefs.

Seen from a greater distance, *Kings or People* reveals the strengths and weaknesses of individualizing comparison. As a way of theorizing, and of illustrating the theory as you go, it works very well. As a way of testing a theory's validity, however, it leaves a great deal to be desired. In fact, the plausibility of the explanations of particular cases arrived at by individualizing comparison depends implicitly on the correctness of general propositions embedded in the explanations. To believe Bendix's account of Germany, for example, we must also believe that, in general, the strength of popular mobilization around a democratic belief varies with the extent of prior articulation of that belief by a strong and unified elite. But that proposition is exactly what remains to be proven!

Again, to accept that "once the English king had been overthrown and parliament was supreme, other monarchies became insecure and the idea of parliamentary government was launched" (Bendix 1978: 250), we must also accept that class struggles within each monarchy fail to explain Europe's successive revolutions and reforms—a proposition left moot by individualizing comparison. In short, individualizing comparison will do to start social inquiry. In the skillful hands of a Bendix, the inquiry will begin very well. Once begun, however, the inquiry that seeks evidence must turn to other sorts of comparison.

6

UNIVERSALIZING COMPARISONS

The Decline of Natural History

For the first half of the twentieth century, social scientists often did their theorizing in the form of standardized "natural histories" of different social phenomena. Individual careers, family lives, communities of a certain type, social movements, revolutions and civilizations all had their own natural histories. The theorist would typically begin with a well-known instance, break the experience of that instance into a sequence of events or a set of stages, then propose the extension of the sequence or stages to many instances—sometimes even to every known instance. The demonstration of the theory's validity then consisted of taking up new cases and showing that the course of events within each of them fit into the proposed scheme. The analyst compared the new cases with the old, but not for the purpose of identifying their particularities. On the contrary: The point was to argue their common properties. The natural history involved a primitive but common form of universalizing comparison.

Natural history cut a wide swathe through social analysis. Analysts proposed natural histories of delinquent careers, of communities, of social movements. They purported to verify those natural-history schemes by showing that the main elements of diverse instances fell into the same sequences. Theories of economic growth and of modernization gave natural history its most prestigious twentieth-century applications. They often took the form of stages: preconditions, takeoff, transition, maturity, and so on. As Sidney Pollard complains:

> . . .we have treated each country like a plant in a separate flower pot, growing independently into a recognizable industrial society according to a genetic code wholly contained in its seed. But this is not how the industrialization of Europe occurred. Rather, it was a single process: the plants had common roots and were subject to a common climate. Further, the development and chronology of the industrial revolution in each area was vitally affected by its place in the general advance, by those ahead of it as well as those trailing behind it, and this relative role must form part of any description or analysis. [Pollard 1973: 637]

Alexander Gerschenkron made a daring, influential innovation: He proposed that the tempo and mechanisms of economic growth varied systematically from "early" to "late" developers; the state, for example, appeared to play a larger and more direct part in the accumulation and investment of capital among the latecomers. Gerschenkron did not, however, abandon the idea of a standard sequence. In his natural history, the species evolved in response to a changing environment.

Almost inevitably, models of modernization in general commonly appeared in natural-history form: stages, sequences, transitions, growth. Thus Clark Kerr theorized about the "commitment" of industrial workers:

> . . .there is a certain "normal" pattern in the process of commitment of workers to industrial life. Four stages may be distinguished, or perhaps it would be more accurate to say that four points may be identified in the continuum of behavioral change which marks the transition of the worker from traditional society to full adherence to the industrial way of life. These four stages may be designated as follows: (1) the uncommitted worker, (2) the semicommitted worker, (3) the committed worker, and (4) the overcommitted worker. [Kerr 1960: 351]

Kerr then built his model as a commentary on the characteristic behavior of workers in each of the four stages. The illustrations did not come from the same workers at different points in their lives, but from different groups of workers: South African gold miners, bachelor workers in Nairobi, and so forth. Kerr's analysis epitomizes the application of natural history to modernization. Such ideas had two attractions: first, to connect changes in communication, family structure, political activity, and any number of other social phenomena with alterations in production; second, to suggest programs of action—speeding up or guiding the process of modernization.

To find natural history credible and useful, one must believe that the social phenomena in question fall into coherent, self-contained clusters; and that change within any particular instance results largely from internal causes. To accept Arnold Toynbee's massive scheme of rise, maturity, and breakdown of civilizations, for example, we must believe that a "civilization" is a self-contained, coherent entity, that each civilization organizes around a fundamental set of values, that people within the civilization gradually exhaust the possibilities within that set of values, and that the exhaustion of values causes transformations in all aspects of civilizations. Toynbee's grand scheme for civilizations belongs to a family of natural histories; Oswald Spengler, Pitirim Sorokin, and Alfred Kroeber all fathered members of the family.

Characteristically, Sorokin criticized his colleagues for treating civilizations as coherent wholes with independent but similar lives. Only integrated systems can change coherently, he taught; the civilizations identified by Spengler, Kroeber, and Toynbee, he claimed, were not integrated systems. But, he thought, "cultural supersystems," integrated by definition, do form and pass through Ideational, Idealistic, and Sensate phases. Having laid out these judgments, Sorokin summarized in superb self-confidence:

Despite the basic misconceptions of the structure and movement of the civilizations which Toynbee, Spengler, and Danilevsky premise for their thinking, certain of their conclusions are nevertheless valid if divorced from their false frame of reference. Reinterpreted and placed within the scheme of sensate, idealistic, and ideational supersystems and less integrated eclectic cultures, they agree essentially with the conclusions of my analysis of these systems and greatly reinforce them. [Sorokin 1947: 643; reading these comments on writers to whom Sorokin was fairly sympathetic, one begins to understand why some of his colleagues in American sociology found him "difficult".]

Although massive schemes in the style of Toynbee or Sorokin have lost favor in the social sciences, natural history was no passing fancy. Eighteenth- and nineteenth-century founders of our social sciences— Vico, Buckle, St. Simon, Comte, Tylor, and Spencer come instantly to mind—often used broad-brush natural history as a theoretical device. Theorists since World War II have generally trimmed their aspirations. Yet natural history has continued to thrive in the form of evolutionary and developmental schemes applied to "societies" rather than civilizations.

Natural history has also found employment on a smaller scale. Crane Brinton, a distinguished intellectual historian, once wrote a little book called *The Anatomy of Revolution*. Although thousands of books and articles on revolution have appeared since the *Anatomy's* appearance in 1938, it is very likely still the best-known general book on the subject in English. Scholars still use it; as recently as 1983, an Iranian historian was pronouncing its central model the best template for the Iranian Revolution of 1979 (Keddie 1983: 590).

What is that model? Contemplating the English, American, French, and Russian revolutions, Brinton offered the metaphor of fever:

In the society during the generation or so before the outbreak of revolution, in the old regime, there will be found signs of the coming disturbance. Rigorously, these signs are not quite symptoms, since when the symptoms are fully enough developed the disease is already present. They are perhaps better described as *prodromal* signs, indications to the very keen diagnostician that a disease is on its way, but not yet sufficiently developed to be the disease. Then comes a time when the full symptoms disclose themselves, and when we can say the fever of revolution has begun. This works up, not regularly but with advances and retreats, to a crisis, frequently accompanied by delirium, the rule of the most violent revolutionists, the Reign of Terror. After the crisis comes a period of convalescence, usually marked by a relapse or two. Finally the fever is over, and the patient is himself again, perhaps in some respects actually strengthened by the experience, immunized at least for a while from a similar attack, but certainly not wholly made over into a new man. The parallel goes through to the end, for societies which undergo the full cycle of revolution are perhaps in some respects the stronger for it; but they by no means emerge entirely remade. [Brinton 1965: 16–17]

Reaching back to medieval tradition, Brinton adopted the image of society as a body. Revolution was a fever that seized the body, then passed. With his customary touch of malice, Brinton self-consciously adopted a metaphor from pathology, then warned his readers that they should not read into the metaphor any hostility to revolution. The bulk of his book went through the postulated stages one by one, illustrating from the histories of all four revolutions.

Although Brinton himself had no trouble distinguishing the English, American, French, and Russian revolutions, his discussion emphasized their similarities. At the end, he sketched "some tentative uniformities." He saw these characteristics, for instance, in all four old regimes:

1 The societies involved were undergoing economic expansion, and participants in their revolutions were not generally miserable.
2 The societies were riven by bitter class antagonisms.
3 Significant numbers of intellectuals had transferred their allegiances away from the regime.
4 The governmental machinery was inefficient.
5 The old ruling classes had lost confidence in themselves and their traditions.

Brinton proposed a series of uniformities for each stage of revolution, with the first phase involving "financial breakdown, organization of the discontented to remedy this breakdown (or threatened breakdown), revolutionary demands on the part of these organized discontented, demands which if granted would mean the virtual abdication of those governing, attempted use of force by the government, its failure, and the attainment of power by the revolutionists" (Brinton 1965: 253). The *Anatomy* offered similar uniformities for each of the subsequent stages: the movement of power among revolutionaries, the rule of extremists, the reaction, and the restoration. With occasional pauses for description, qualification, and reflection, the book pursued uniformities.

Brinton's natural history mixed sense and nonsense. He knew the events of the four revolutions (especially the French Revolution, on which he had earlier written a monograph) well. As a result, he was able to describe features of each revolution that fit his scheme. His emphasis on the vulnerablility of the states involved caught an element that other natural histories, focused too intently on revolutionaries alone, missed.

Brinton's fever metaphor, however, confused the issue. Despite all the qualifications he attached to it, the idea of fever suggests that a revolution happens to something like a single person—to a society personified. That suggestion wipes away the struggle of parties, the play of coalitions, the problem of seizing control of a governmental structure, reshaping it, and subjecting other people to its force. It locates the revolution in the revolutionary elites. Finally, it relegates ordinary people to a chorus: either following the soloists' lead or standing silent.

The last few decades' historiography of all four revolutions, with its rediscovery of party struggle and popular participation, has made Brinton's account obsolete. Even quite conventional histories of the American Revolution, for example, now make room for the partly autonomous involvement of shopkeepers and artisans in the struggles with Britain. Recent writing on the Russian Revolution and its antecedents, likewise, presents urban workers as organized and class conscious. The work of such scholars as Christopher Hill gives the English Revolution a popular base far wider than the division between King and Parliament suggests. And studies of the French Revolution, beginning with Georges Lefebvre's *Paysans du Nord*, have led the way to an understanding of popular participation in revolutionary struggles throughout Europe. Although the place of class struggle in the American, English, Russian, and French Revolution remains hotly contested, no scheme that ignores popular politics can now stand up against the evidence.

Models of Revolution

Indeed, the trend in revolutionary historiography seems to have discouraged the construction of natural histories. Models of revolution continue to proliferate, but proposals of standard sequences become rarer and rarer. Increasingly, self-consciously constructed models of revolution (as opposed to the implicit schemes people use when interpreting particular revolutions) concern (1) causes and precipitating conditions, (2) alignments of classes and parties, (3) mobilization and demobilization, and (4) outcomes. This does not mean, however, the universalizing comparison has disappeared. On the contrary: It has become increasingly common to defend models of revolution by lining up several instances in which revolution did occur and stressing their common properties.

Take James Davies' influential J-curve model as a case in point. (Davies authorizes our making a connection between him and Crane Brinton by dedicating his reader *When Men Revolt and Why* to Brinton: "He never fathered a revolution but he articulated its anatomy in our disjointed time.") As Davies summarizes his argument:

The thesis is a fundamentally psychological one, referring to individuals rather than social aggregates: revolution is most likely to occur when a long period of rising expectations and gratifications is followed by a period during which gratifications (socioeconomic and otherwise) suddenly drop off while expectations (socioeconomic or otherwise) continue to rise. The rapidly widening gap between expectations and gratifications portends revolution. The most common case [sic] for this widening gap of individual dissatisfactions is economic or social dislocation that makes the affected individual generally tense, generally frustrated. That is, the greatest portion of people who join a revolution are preoccupied with tensions related to the failure to gratify the physical (economic) needs and the needs for stable interpersonal (social) relationships. [Davies 1971: 133]

In his original presentation of the model (1962), Davies proposed it as an alternative to the ideas that revolutions result from misery or progressive degradation. No, said he: Rising expectations, disappointed by a downturn, open the way to revolution. Davies shared that general view with Tocqueville, Brinton, and a number of relative-deprivation theorists. Davies centered his analysis on individual psychology more clearly and completely than the rest. In offering Dorr's Rebellion, the Russian Revolution of 1917, and the Egyptian Revolution of 1952 as confirming examples, he also wrote as if an angry public were the essential ingredient of revolution.

Davies compounded that impression by extending the J-curve formulation, with less documentation, to Leisler's Rebellion of 1689, the American Revolution, the French Revolution, the New York draft riots of 1863, and the riots of Nyasaland in 1959. (Later, he added the American Civil War, the Nazi seizure of power, and the movement of American blacks in the 1960s: Davies 1979.) In passing, he disposed of the one negative case on his roster—the revolution that failed to occur during the American depression of the 1930s—by invoking the rapid, vigorous intervention of the federal government. Thus Davies made clear that he was trying to state the conditions under which large numbers of people become angry enough to attack their government.

In the 1971 reprinting, Davies added a qualification: "But socioeco-nomically deprived poor people are unlikely to make a successful rebellion, a revolution, by themselves. Their discontent needs the addition of the discontents developing among individuals in the mid-dle class and the ruling class when they are rather suddenly deprived (socioeconomically or otherwise)" (Davies 1971: 133). Nevertheless, the qualified model continued to treat the amount of discontent in a population as the prime determinant of rebellion en masse, and to propose that a J-curve pattern of expectations and achievements pushes the amount of discontent above the threshold.

Notice what Davies did **not** do. He did not compare his supposedly confirming cases with other similar cases in which revolutions failed to occur. With the exception of the American Depression, he did not look for instances in which J-curves appeared without revolution. He provided no rule for deciding which satisfactions are crucial when some are being frustrated and others not. Nor did he specify, much less verify, the presumed links from the J-curve of satisfactions to the necessary discontent, or from the discontent to the seizure of power. He did not meet the conditions Morris Zelditch has listed for intelli-gible comparison: no method of differences, no elimination of third variables, and so on. In a universalizing mood, he compared a number of instances to a model and claimed to have discovered a correspon-dence.

None of those failures disproves the J-curve model. Short of doing the missing work ourselves—a thankless task—we will be unable to refute it. My own sense of the evidence runs strongly against the model, on two grounds: **first,** that people's rising expectations are being disappointed all the time without revolution, and such time series analyses as we have available for a wide variety of conflicts point away from the expected pattern; **second,** that whether widespread discontent actually couples with a revolutionary situation depends on structural circumstances that have little or no connection with the generality of discontent. Those "structural circumstances" include the military vulnerability of the state, the internal organization of its opposition, and the character of coalitions among classes.

Theda Skocpol's Revolutions

Lest anyone conclude that universalizing comparisons of revolutions inevitably lead to unsatisfactory models and neglect of structure, let us look at a remarkably successful deployment of the universalizing logic. If anyone emphasizes structural circumstances favoring revolutions, Theda Skocpol is the one.

Skocpol's *States and Social Revolutions* sets up a sustained comparison of the French, Russian, and Chinese revolutions. It seeks to identify the necessary and sufficient conditions of genuine social revolutions: those that rapidly transform state and class structures. More precisely, it attacks the explanation of the subclass of social revolutions that occur in rich, noncolonial agrarian bureaucracies, as a first step toward explaining social revolutions in general.

As Lewis Coser says, Skocpol "sets herself resolutely against any psychological explanations of revolutionary developments in terms of the frustrations or relative deprivation of the underlying population. She contends instead that only structural explanations allow one to reach an explanation of the causes of revolution" (Coser 1979: 13). Discontents, even intense discontents, occur widely in history, but social revolutions hardly ever happen; the problem, concludes Skocpol, is to identify those rare structural conditions that permit existing discontents to coalesce in revolutionary action.

In many respects, Skocpol wrote her own version of the book her teacher, Barrington Moore, Jr., was writing at the same time. Moore's earlier *Social Origins of Dictatorship and Democracy* had included sustained treatments of the French and Chinese revolutions, as well as using the Russian Revolution of 1917 as a foil for the analysis of China. But despite scrutinizing each revolution carefully for evidence of the conflicts and class alignments prevailing in each country, the Moore of *Social Origins* finally presented the revolutions as expressions of changes in class structure that were already under way. Temporary coalitions of classes, each having solid material reasons for opposition to the ruling classes and their states, made revolutions.

That conclusion, satisfactory for most purposes of *Social Origins*, called up a thorny question: Since many, many people have solid material reasons for opposition to ruling classes and their states, why do major rebellions occur seldom and transforming revolutions almost never?

Moore first mentioned the question in a commentary on the Terror in France:

As the victims of the September massacres show—mainly poor people who happened to be in jail when the mob burst in—popular resentments could erupt in sudden acts of indiscriminate vengeance. Nevertheless, a dispassionate analysis cannot just draw back in horror at this point; it is necessary to perceive the causes. They are clear enough in the aggravating circumstances of the moment and the history of degradation and oppression to which the mass of people at the very bottom of the social order were subject. To express outrage at the September massacres and forget the horrors behind them is to indulge in a partisan trick. In that sense there is no mystery here. In another there is. As we shall see most clearly later, when we come to consider India, severe suffering does not always and necessarily generate revolutionary outbursts, and certainly not a revolutionary situation. That problem must wait. [Moore 1966: 101]

The problem did wait. Although Moore did consider the causes and costs of nonrevolution in India later in *Social Origins*, the problem of necessary and sufficient causes of popular rebellion appeared in that book only intermittently. It finally reappeared in his book *Injustice* almost fifteen years later.

As Moore left the question at the close of *Social Origins*, he could go in either of two directions: toward the general structural conditions under which aggrieved people could actually seize power or toward the circumstances in which people who had solid material reasons for grievance actually articulated those grievances and acted on them. He feinted in the first direction, but followed through in the second. His book *Injustice* did deal with "suppressed historical alternatives," such as the development of durable socialist power in Germany, and did reason about why those possibilities did not materialize. But its chief itinerary led through the conditions in which people define the behavior of powerful others as unjust, via the relationship between the sense of injustice and participation in determined, collective opposition. That exploration took him past a rich variety of experiences, movements, and political forms, but few revolutions.

Theda Skocpol took the other path. She deliberately focused on indisputably great revolutions, intentionally examined the social structures behind those great revolutions with care, self-consciously compared the social structures and the revolutions point by point. Where Moore treated existing states as relatively direct expressions of the interests of a dominant class or class coalition at the states' formative moments, she meant to give the structure of the state full, independent weight. An "organizational-realist" view of the state, she said, informed her work (Skocpol 1979: 31).

Skocpol has written many analyses of states and revolutions and taken more than one perspective on them. Let us concentrate here on the perspective of her major treatment of the subject, *States and Social Revolutions*. In that book, Skocpol's comparisons appeared in three different configurations:

1 social revolutions *vs.* nonrevolutions: (France + Russia + China) *vs.* (Japan + Prussia);
2 revolutionary country *vs.* closely matched nonrevolutionary country: (France *vs.* England), (Russia 1917 *vs.* Russia 1905), (China *vs.* Japan);
3 revolutionary countries compared: France *vs.* Russia *vs.* China.

Japan, Prussia, England, and Russia 1905 entered the analysis as other countries, similar to the featured three, which failed to have social revolutions.

In her book's first half, Skocpol emphasizes common properties. In the second, she spends a great deal of her effort establishing particularities of France, Russia 1917, and China. There are moments, then, when her comparisons serve mainly to individualize. If *States and Social Revolutions* assigned equal weight to the three sets of comparisons, we could reasonably push the book over from universalizing toward variation-finding comparison. Three features of the analysis, however, give it a universalizing air. First, although she recognized a large class of social revolutions, Skocpol chose to concentrate on the subclass of social revolutions occurring within agrarian bureaucracies. She chose to do so on the precise ground that "France, Russia, and

China exhibited important similarities in their Old Regimes and revolutionary processes and outcomes—similarities more than sufficient to
warrant their treatment together as one pattern calling for a coherent
causal explanation" (Skocpol 1979: 41). Second, she used the comparisons among France, Russia, and China almost exlusively to identify similarities in their circumstances, rather than to discover principles of variation. "France, Russia, and China," she remarked,

will serve as three positive cases of successful social revolution, and I shall
argue that these cases reveal similar causal patterns despite their many other
differences. In addition, I shall invoke negative cases for the purpose of
validating various particular parts of the causal argument. [Skocpol 1979: 37]

She was quite aware of differences among the countries, both in the
settings of their revolutions and in the courses of the revolutions themselves. But she sought chiefly to identify their common properties and
to track them to common causes.

The stress on common causes brings us to the third point. The
comparisons of France, Russia 1917, and China with Japan, Prussia,
England, and Russia 1905 occupied a distinctly minor position in the
analysis as a whole. As Skocpol herself commented in a later essay on
comparative history, in *States and Social Revolutions* "only the 'positive' cases of social revolution receive extensive discussion. 'Negative'—or control—cases are discussed much less fully. For they are
introduced strictly for the purpose of helping to validate the main
argument about the causes of social revolutions in France, Russia, and
China" (Skocpol and Somers 1980: 185).

Skocpol arrived at this sort of comparison because she sought "valid,
complete explanations of revolutions" (Skocpol 1979: 5). Furthermore, she had a particular understanding of what it means to explain
revolutions; explanation consists of identifying the necessary, and if
possible the sufficient, conditions for a rare, complex event: a rapid,
basic transformation of a society's state and class structures, accompanied and in part carried through by class-based revolts from below.
In searching for causes of revolution, she explicitly invoked John
Stuart Mill's Method of Agreement and Method of Difference; those
are ways of identifying the uniquely determining causes of a phenomenon. In so doing, she implicitly rejected the procedure which social
scientists confronted with an explanatory problem more commonly

employ: placing the critical instances to be explained within a field of variation, identifying correlates of the crucial variation, then attempting—via another version of the Methods of Agreement and Difference—to sort out the causal priorities among those correlates.

Skocpol also eschewed more modest programs of explanation. Other analysts of revolution have, for example, taken explanation to consist of accounting convincingly for the courses of events—including the success or failure of revolutionary movements—in different revolutionary situations or reliably identifying the relationships among circumstances before, during, and after different revolutions. Neither of these requires a specification of necessary and sufficient conditions for successful social revolutions.

Because she adopted an extremely demanding program of explanation, Skocpol vigorously rejected any attempt to "explain" revolutions by comparing them with other forms of conflict. Likewise, she would have nothing to do with "purposive" accounts starting from the interests and organization of various revolutionary actors. No explanation of social revolutions that merely accounted for some of their features—for example, the more direct involvement of some classes than others—would satisfy her. Her search for a "valid, complete" explanation of social revolutions, then, embodied an exceptionally ambitious program of explanation. Unlike most other social scientists, she would not settle for explaining some significant part of the variance.

Skocpol's zealous explanatory program couples with a determination to bring politics back into the analysis of large-scale social changes. By politics she means the organization and use of coercion, especially in the form of national states. That insistence on politics shows up repeatedly in the detail of *States and Social Revolutions;* Skocpol attributes considerable importance, for example, to village power structure in accounting for agrarian rebellions in France, Russia, and China.

Indeed, Skocpol could have strengthened her analysis by examining variation in revolutionary activity from one type of village to another **within** France, Russia, and China. In her treatment, for example, France appears as a country with relatively backward agriculture (Europe's only more advanced case, England, serving as the criterion) and solidary peasant villages. What is more, she minimizes the importance of regional variation. "Regional variations in combinations of community structures, landholding patterns, forms of rent extraction, and eighteenth-century socioeconomic trends," she remarks,

> were apparently not very important in determining the general shape and incidence of peasant revolts in 1789 (however much they may have had to do with which particular grievances were emphasized and which specific targets were attacked by individual peasant communities). What happened after 1788 was spurred by a *national* political crisis into which peasants everywhere— those with potential as well as actual grievances—were drawn through almost simultaneous, kingdom-wide events such as the drawing up of the *cahiers* and the Municipal Revolution. The peasant rebellion was indeed autonomous and spontaneous—but only within this national context. Peasant actions in 1789 thus cannot be understood merely as extensions of "subterranean" struggles carried on in localities throughout the eighteenth century. [Skocpol 1979: 125]

Skocpol has a point, but she carries it too far. She is quite right to stress the visible vulnerability of the French state as an encouragement to rural action in 1789. But from that point on, the simplifications of French historians—such as the Georges Lefebvre of *The Coming of the French Revolution*—mislead her.

In fact, rural France of the eighteenth century embraced regions variously dominated by small-holding peasants, sharecroppers, large commercial farms with agricultural wage-labor, small merchants running cottage industry, rack-renting landlords, rapacious monasteries, and combinations of the six. Their village structures varied in rough conformity to the organization of production. In 1789, the intensity and character of rural conflict varied greatly from one region to another; only the lumping of struggle for control of food (characteristically a concern of rural proletarians) with attacks on landlords (characteristically a concern of smallholders, tenants, and squatters who were being squeezed by capitalizing and enclosing landowners) into the category of "peasant revolt" keeps the variation from being obvious.

The cash-crop farming of France's Flanders, for example, drew admiration from all who saw it, including English agrarian observer Arthur Young. Yet it divided the rural population into large peasants, smallholders, tenants, and a large number of wage-workers who split their time between manufacturing and agricultural labor. In 1789, Flanders plunged into the "peasant revolt," but its wage-workers generally struggled over food supply, while smallholders and tenants went after noble and ecclesiastical landlords.

Languedoc followed a different path. By 1789 Upper Languedoc's landlords had been working for about a century to convert their region into a "wheat machine" and their tenants into dependent wage-laborers; the process was incomplete, however, and some villages had retained considerable autonomy. In Upper Languedoc, "peasant revolt" stopped sooner and threatened less than in Flanders, but it most often took the form of repossessing use rights which landlords had eliminated. In Lower Languedoc, a region of small-holding, herding, and extensive cottage industry, the major conflicts of the early Revolution set Catholic workers against Protestant entrepreneurs.

In Anjou, the wine-, wheat-, and flax-growing areas near the Loire supported thoroughly commercialized cash-crop agriculture, with smallholders, tenants, and wage-laborers cheek by jowl with ecclesiastical landlords and tithe-collectors. Away from the river much of the countryside broke up into medium-sized farms owned by noble or ecclesiastical landlords but operated by long-term tenants with a certain amount of capital, who drew some seasonal labor from the many land-poor or landless people engaged in cottage textile production. Although Anjou's greatest concentrations of wage-workers struggled over the food supply in 1789, nothing one could reasonably call a "peasant revolt" occurred there.

In all these regions the conflicts of 1789 were "subterranean" in the sense that they brought into the open struggles that had begun long before, but which authorities and landlords had been better able to contain before 1789. And in all these regions the failing efforts of local authorities to suppress the various forms of rural conflict typically precipitated seizures of power in the name of a revolutionary committee. Attacks on noble and ecclesiastical landlords—rare indeed in the seventeenth century—had been multiplying during the eighteenth century in regions of expanding agrarian capitalism. Likewise, struggles over food had been increasing as wage-labor expanded in grain-shipping regions.

In these ways, the rural conflicts of 1789 had a certain autonomy. The fiscal crisis, the struggle with the Parlements, and the calling of the Estates General surely increased the vulnerability of royal authorities to attack. They increased the likelihood of simultaneous resistance to royal power in different sections of the countryside. Yet the uneven distribution of rural struggles against capitalist aggrandizement itself favored social revolution. It meant that in some regions the revolutionary bourgeoisie found strong rural allies—smallholders and wage-workers alike—against landlords and royal officials. If France had consisted mainly of solidary peasant villages whose people were eager to throw off their exploiters, the coalition of merchants, lawyers, and other bourgeois who actually constituted the revolutionary network of 1789 would never have managed their repeated seizures of local power; the bourgeois were too clearly identified with the peasants' exploiters.

That much calls one part of Skocpol's argument into question. She minimizes variation from one rural area to another, stresses the widespread predominance of a peasantry organized in solidary communities, and treats a general reaction to seigneurial exploitation as the incentive to "peasant" uprisings in 1789. Instead, sharp regional variation in rural social structure, frequent resistance to the expansion of agrarian capitalism, and deep divisions among cash-crop farmers, agricultural proletarians, and true peasants facilitated the victory of a bourgeois coalition. The coalition had its own political constituency in some regions and was able to borrow outside force in others.

Yet, properly understood, the variety of rural conflicts actually strengthens Skocpol's overall analysis. For it explains how a series of rural rebellions that were sometimes antiseigneurial, sometimes anticapitalist, and sometimes both could favor a bourgeois revolution. It establishes that the declining ability of capitalizing landlords and merchants to call on the state's agents for support in the face of resistance and rebellion actually facilitated the revolutionary transfer of power. A bit more concern with the local ramifications of national politics would have made these conditions clearer.

Skocpol's concern to put national politics at the center shows up especially in her general argument. That argument makes revolution mainly a function of the inability of threatened national states to act. Here is a compact statement of her thesis:

. . .in late-eighteenth-century France, early-twentieth-century Russia, and mid-nineteenth through early-twentieth-century China alike, the monarchies of the Old Regimes proved unable to implement sufficiently basic reforms or to promote rapid enough economic development to meet and weather the particular intensity of military threats from abroad that each regime had to face. And revolutionary crises emerged precisely because of the unsuccessful attempts of the Bourbon, Romanov, and Manchu regimes to cope with foreign pressures. Institutional relationships existed between the monarchs and their staffs, on the one hand, and the agrarian economies, on the other hand, that made it impossible for the imperial states to cope successfully with competition or intrusions from abroad. As a result, the Old Regimes either were dissolved through the impact of defeat in total war with more developed powers (i.e. Russia) or were deposed at home through the reaction of politically powerful landed upper classes against monarchical attempts to mobilize resources or impose reforms (i.e. France and China). Either way, the upshot was the disintegration of centralized administrative machineries that had theretofore provided the sole unified bulwark of social and political order. No longer reinforced by the prestige and coercive power of autocratic monarchy, the existing class relations became vulnerable to assaults from below. [Skocpol 1979: 50–51]

Note that the statement includes a certain amount of logical curve-fitting, similar in function to Robert Hamblin's insertion of empirically estimated exponents in his general equations for social change: Total war, for example, becomes the equivalent of resistance by domestic landed classes, and "assaults from below" cover a variety of evils.

These reservations aside, are the main lines of Skocpol's description correct? Did the old regimes of China, Russia, and France, hampered by existing relationships between their central authorities and their agrarian economies, weaken in the course of failed responses to foreign pressures, dissolve through challenges from more powerful states and/or their own landed upper classes, become vulnerable to assaults from below, and succumb when those assaults actually materialized?

Except for the strictly contingent role attributed to rural action against the state and the ruling class, this summary is at least defensible in the present state of scholarship on China, Russia, and France. To be sure, a William Doyle could complain that the parallel equates the relatively minor international difficulties of eighteenth-century France with the enormous vulnerability of Russia and China and slights the importance of divisions within France's ruling elite; a Victoria Bonnell could argue the importance of organized urban workers in the making of the Russian revolutionary crisis; a Ralph Thaxton could maintain that a folk revolutionary tradition played a powerful, autonomous part in the development of the Chinese revolution. Nevertheless, in its own broad terms Skocpol's summary does identify common properties of the three states and their revolutions.

Does Skocpol's statement present the necessary and sufficient conditions for social revolution? Is it true that "(1) state organizations susceptible to administrative and military collapse when subjected to intensified pressures from more developed countries abroad and (2) agrarian sociopolitical structures that facilitated widespread peasant revolts against landlords were, taken together, the sufficient distinctive causes of social-revolutionary situations commencing in France, 1789, Russia, 1917, and China, 1911" (Skocpol 1979: 154)?

Aye, there's the rub: In fitting her summary so tightly to the common circumstances of three countries at critical moments of their histories, Skocpol has weakened her own effort to construct "valid, complete" explanations for social revolutions in agrarian bureaucracies. It is always possible to invoke one more circumstance the three states had in common: their increasing implication in the world capitalist economy, the growing importance of their merchants, the shift of their landlords toward greater profit-making, the inefficiency of their fiscal systems, and others besides. How do we know that these factors don't belong among the "sufficient distinctive causes"? If causes interact (for instance, if structures facilitating widespread peasant revolts only matter in the presence of aggrandizing landlords), one-variable comparisons with other similar countries cannot rule out the necessity of these additional causes.

We should, however, distinguish between Skocpol's self-conscious design of the analysis and her detailed treatment of the cases at hand. Within her basic design, Skocpol failed to take advantage of the fact of variation. As Randall Collins puts it:

She excepts cases like seventeenth century England, or nineteenth century Prussia or Japan because they did not undergo social as well as political transformations; in fact, precisely for this reason she is able to use them as test cases, and thus show how the military crisis must be combined with an internal mass revolt if a social revolution is to follow. But this is really only a form of exposition. A theory of revolutions should be a theory of the conditions for various kinds of revolutions, and Skocpol herself has stated some of the key determinants of the variants just mentioned. [Collins 1980: 651]

In actual practice, Skocpol recognizes the differences among her cases and begins to weave analyses of their variation. When dealing with China, for example, she begins to connect the greater prerevolutionary autonomy of landlords and warlords, the wider sweep of peasant rebellion, the more extensive involvement of peasant-backed revolutionaries, and the creation of a transforming populist regime.

Even if we grant validity to Skocpol's most general summary of the three revolutions, therefore, we have room to look at systematic differences among them, and to convert those differences into tentative generalizations. For example, the extent to which a state's military force remains intact and unified probably affects both the likelihood of revolution and the extent of which those who control the revolutionary state can contain their rivals and opponents; in that respect, the differences among France, Russia, and China look promising. Likewise, the comparisons with Prussia, England, Japan, and Russia 1905 have more to give. We might look, for instance, at the relationship between the extent of articulation among those who control the means of production and of coercion, on the one hand, and the inclination toward revolutions from above, on the other. In short, shift from either/or to in-so-far-as.

A shift of this kind means a move away from universalizing comparison. It means emphasizing variations among social revolutions. It means moving toward either variation-finding comparison (establishing a principle of variation in the character or intensity of a phenomenon by examining systematic differences among instances) or encompassing comparison (placing different instances at various locations within the same system, explaining their characteristics as a function of their varying relationships to the system as a whole). The next two chapters will give us an opportunity to weigh the costs and benefits of such a move.

7

FINDING VARIATION

How and When to Look for Variation

If we believed textbooks and learned essays on the subject, almost all valid comparison would be variation-finding: comparison establishing a principle of variation in the character or intensity of a phenomenon having more than one form by examining systematic differences among instances. In fact, perfectly sound varieties of individualizing, universalizing, and encompassing comparisons exist. The advantage of variation-finding comparison is parsimony: a successful comparison in this mode produces a principle that extends readily to new cases, yet is relatively easy to verify, falsify, or modify on the basis of the new evidence.

Those attractions have, unhappily, tempted social scientists into some of their greatest technical abuses. There is the abuse of the Great Blender, in which we take numerical observations on a hundred-odd national states, made comparable by the magic fact of appearing in parallel columns of a statistical handbook, and run multiple regressions or factor analyses in order to discern the dimensions of development, of modernity, of political instability, or of some other equally ill-defined global concept. There is the abuse of the Ersatz Laboratory, in which survey teams establish themselves in a number of different countries, translate a common questionnaire into the various local languages, send out interviewers to ask the questions of presumably comparable samples of individuals or households in each country, code up their results into standard categories, then pool the information thus manufactured into an analysis of cross-cultural variation in the relationship between X and Y, with Z controlled. Let us not forget the abuse of the Cultural Checkerboard, in which hired graduate students read stacks of ethnographic articles and monographs, recording for each "society" encountered the presence or absence of patrilocal residence, early weaning, male puberty rituals, couvade, and dozens of other cultural traits, then transform their judgments into holes in Hollerith cards, so that someone else can run statistical analyses to determine either which "societies" resemble each other most, or which cultural traits vary together. We encountered examples of some of these abuses in examining the fallacious idea of social change as a coherent general phenomenon. I will not inflict any more dreary examples on you.

Not that all quantitative comparisons abuse the truth. Despite the misleading narrowness of the activities it quantifies, national income analysis has given us precious insights into worldwide variation in economic activity. We would understand much less of the world's population dynamics if demographers had not invented standard descriptions of vital rates and assembled relatively comparable series of measurements for many states. Censuses, for all their weaknesses, remain a precious source of evidence concerning international differences in labor force participation, living conditions, household structure, and age distributions. In principle, the pooling of administratively generated statistics, the conduct of comparable surveys (including censuses) in several different countries, and the coding of ethnographers' observations provide a sense of systematic variation that tempers the temptation to take the round we live each day as the measure of the entire world. The international standardization of time-budget surveys that began in the 1960s, for example, makes it clear how extensively citizens of the rich western countries, and especially the United States, are substituting television time for work time. That is an important phenomenon, better established by quantitative comparison.

My claims, then, are not that quantification is worthless, that international comparisons are bootless, that surveys and ethnographers al-

ways lie. I claim instead that variation-finding comparisons become
more dangerous and less valuable to the extent that:

1   The arguments being examined are loosely specified or unstated;
    for example, the study explores for a general relationship between
    development (loosely specified) and political participation (loosely
    specified).
2   The relations among the units differ from those specified by the
    arguments being examined; for example, the argument specifies a
    developmental sequence, while the data concern a sample of na-
    tional states observed at the same point in time.
3   The comparisons treat many units whose comparability with re-
    spect to the questions being asked is uncertain; for example, a study
    of industrialization and family structure uses observations on all
    states appearing in the *United Nations Demographic Yearbook*.
4   They treat many units whose independence with respect to the
    characteristics being measured is uncertain; for example, Belgium,
    Luxembourg, the Netherlands, The German Federal Republic,
    Switzerland, France, and Liechtenstein appear as separate cases in
    an analysis of the relationship between television viewing and
    newspaper readership.
5   The concern relationships among many measured characteristics
    whose comparability with respect to the arguments being examined
    is uncertain; for example, proportion of the population voting in
    national elections is used as a measure of intensity of political
    participation, without allowance for variations in registration re-
    quirements or in the actual significance of elections as a way of
    gaining or losing power.
6   Measurements of those characteristics combine different levels of
    aggregation whose pertinence to the arguments being examined
    varies; for example, some observations (such as the size of the
    national army) refer to the state, while others (such as the crime
    rate) refer to an aggregation from individual events.
7   Measurements of those characteristics rest on the judgments of
    people who are unfamiliar with the overall structures of those
    units; for example, student assistants sort occupational titles from
    multiple countries into twelve identical categories.
8   The judgments in question aggregate complex, concrete observa-
    tions into simple, abstract categories; for example, those students
    must judge whether opposition parties exist or do not exist.

9   The analytical procedures compare the observations for the units
    in question with models assuming (a) well-defined independent
    units, (b) independently-observed characteristics of those units, (c)
    linear covariation of those characteristics; for example, the inves-
    tigator uses multiple regression of untransformed variables mea-
    sured for states belonging to the United Nations to estimate rela-
    tionships among characteristics of societies.

Translated into a positive mood, these stipulations yield the following
rules for effective generalizing comparison: (1) Specify your arguments;
(2) observe units that correspond to the units of your argument; (3)
make sure your units are comparable with respect to the terms of your
argument; (4) either observe units you can reasonably consider to be
independent of each other or make specific allowance for their interdependence in the specification of the argument and the analysis of the
evidence; (5) make your measures correspond closely to the terms of
your argument; (6) either have all your measures pertain to the same
level of aggregation, or subdivide argument and analysis by levels of
aggregation; (7) when a significant element of judgment enters the
coding of evidence, do the coding yourself or test its reliability with
great care; (8) minimize and delay the reduction of detail to abstract
categories; if possible, make that reduction part of the analysis itself; (9)
adopt or devise models corresponding closely to the logic of your
argument.
    Stated positively, then, these principles look a lot like ordinary re-
searchers' common sense. Yet very few comparative studies meet these
standards, and many fall far short. The effort of undertaking proper
specification and measurement seems to intimidate the great bulk of
comparative social researchers. Hence my complaints.

Barrington Moore Compares

Barrington Moore offered a precocious example of the turn to seriously
historical comparisons concerning small numbers of crucial experiences. The success of his historical venture encouraged others to fol-

low his road. *Social Origins of Dictatorship and Democracy* is one of those works that sets the style and object of inquiry for a generation of researchers. At the time of its appearance, Lawrence Stone (not a man given to awarding medals for trivial performances) called *Social Origins* a "flawed masterpiece" (Stone 1967: 34). Flawed, Stone thought, because the book treated the authoritarianism of Japan and Germany as a long-term characteristic rather than a passing phase, because it exaggerated the significance of violence in history, because it underestimated the influence of ideology, because it insisted on the transforming effect of the American Civil War, because it accepted the old coercive account of English enclosures, and because of a series of lesser failings. Nevertheless, said Stone,

no one has ever before tried to use the comparative method on such a scale, and with so careful a study of the professional literature. Few have ever before defined so clearly the importance of the peasantry in a revolution, or the political significance of whether the alliance of landlords and industrialists is formed under the patronage of the state or in opposition to it. Few historians treat those with whom they disagree with the generosity and honesty displayed by Moore. Few historians show such respect and admiration for humane and liberal values. [Stone 1967: 34]

Stone's major criticisms of Moore are debatable. Although the English enclosures took longer than Moore's brief discussion suggests, for instance, they certainly involved widespread coercion—especially if we include not only smallholders, but also various kinds of tenants and squatters. Stone's final tribute to Moore's strenuous integrity is not debatable. Barrington Moore laid down a granite slab on which others still build.

Moore set down his slab over three main questions: (1) Given a range of contemporary regimes running from democratic to authoritarian, what features of a country's past determined where in that range it arrived? (2) What role did the landed classes—especially lords and peasants—play in the character and outcomes of the great revolutions? (3) What changes in the countryside opened the way to the various forms of mass politics? The questions obviously interlock. Moore made them perfectly interdependent by asking how the fates of lords and peasants in the course of expansion of capitalist property relations in the countryside and great revolutions affected the subsequent politics of the world's major states.

Roughly speaking, Moore broke the states he considered seriously into four categories, according to their twentieth-century destinations:

- various degrees of capitalist democracy: the United States, England, France;
- different varieties of fascism: Germany, Japan;
- different varieties of socialism: Russia, China;
- stalled democracy, democratic forms without effective representation: India.

Thus Moore simplified his task by consolidating his observations into three or four categories; he made no claim of accounting for the full range of political experiences. To put it more schematically than Moore himself ever cared to, **capitalist democracy** resulted from bourgeois revolutions that transformed or liquidated the old landed classes, **fascism** grew from the development of capitalism with a relatively weak bourgeoisie and without a liquidation of the old landed classes, **socialism** developed from the stifling of commercial and industrial growth by an agrarian bureaucracy which ultimately succumbed to peasant rebellion, and **stalled democracy** appeared through the failure of serious rural transformation.

Moore had originally planned to include sustained separate treatments of Germany and Russia. He finally abandoned that project, but incorporated numerous short comparisons with Germany and Russia into the argument. As a result, the systematic comparison actually proceeded on two levels: democracies/Japan/China/India and United States/England/France. Thus, for example, he argued that the greater fragility of representation in France corresponded to the incomplete liquidation of the Old Regime's landed classes, especially the peasantry.

A third comparison, of a different sort, hovered behind these two. Moore asked what difference the timing of the different forms of transition to modern politics made to the character of the transition. In general, he argued, the democratic transitions cleared the way to the fascist transitions, and the two together—in the guise of the two sorts of states created by the transitions—facilitated the later socialist transitions. (This timetable requires us to see the lineaments of right authoritarianism, if not of fascism *stricto sensu*, in the nineteenth-century German and Japanese regimes. Lawrence Stone's criticism refers to this feature of Moore's argument.) While Moore treated each of his major cases at length in its own terms, comparisons in time and space constituted the book's skeleton.

Several features of the comparisons left something to be desired. Moore discussed Germany, Japan, India, the United States, Russia, China, England, and France as though they were all well-defined, autonomous societies, each having a history that could be explained in its own terms. He bypassed the difficulty of connecting the history of the Prussian state (the center of his treatment of "Germany") and the later Nazi seizure of the German Republic. He wrote rather freely of the "modernization" of the countryside in most of the countries, presenting it as a similar experience with very different political consequences. Indeed, he assumed that the tendency to "modernize" was very general; the question was not whether productive, commercialized agriculture would develop in one country after another, but under whose auspices and with what political outcomes. To my mind, these are mistakes. At a minimum, they need more justification than Moore gave them.

At times, Moore veered in the direction of individualizing comparison, trying to get the particularities right, and using the contrast with a second country mainly for that purpose. A comparison of China and Japan runs:

Thus the feudal military tradition in Japan provided at first a congenial basis for a reactionary version of industrialization, though in the long run it may turn out to have been fatal. In China's pre-modern society and culture there was as little or no basis out of which a militarist patriotism of the Japanese type could grow. In comparison with Japan, the reactionary nationalism of Chiang Kai-shek seems thin and watery. Only when China began to make over her own institutions in the communist image did a strong sense of mission appear. [Moore 1966: 252]

But it is not long before Moore returns to seeking variation on a grand scale:

Hence not feudalism itself, certainly not feudalism as a disembodied general category, holds the key to the way in which Japanese society entered the modern era. To feudalism one must add the distinct factor of timing. Sec-

ondly, it was Japan's particular variety of feudalism with substantial bureaucratic elements that made possible the leap. The special character of the
Japanese feudal bond, with its much greater emphasis on status and military
loyalty than on a freely chosen contractual relationship, meant that one
source of the impetus behind the Western variety of free institutions was
absent. Again, the bureaucratic element in the Japanese policy produced its
characteristic result of a tame and timid bourgeoisie unable to challenge the
old order. The reasons for the absence of a serious intellectual challenge lie
deeper in Japanese history but are part of the same phenomenon. The intellectual and social challenges that made the Western bourgeois revolutions
were feeble to nonexistent. Finally, and perhaps most important of all,
throughout the transition and on into the era of industrial society, the dominant classes were able to contain and deflect disruptive forces arising out of
the peasants. Not only was there no bourgeois revolution, there was also no
peasant revolution. [Moore 1966: 253–54]

Here we catch Moore in the act of joining his particular historical
analysis of Japan to his general scheme. Ideology and political organization, clearly influential in the particular shape of Japan's experience,
disappear as independent causes. The formulas appear: extent of
bourgeois revolution—extent of parliamentary democracy; extent of
peasant revolution—extent of socialist bureaucracy. When, for example, Moore considers the consequences of a nobility's successful
resistance to royal authorities in the absence of a strong bourgeoisie, he
concludes that the outcome "is highly unfavorable to the Western
version of democracy" (Moore 1966: 418). Then he reflects on the
contrast in this regard between Prussia and England:

While absolutism was growing stronger in France, in a large section of Germany, and in Russia, it met its first major check on English soil, where to be
sure the attempt to establish it was much feebler. In very large measure this is
true because the English landed aristocracy at an early date began to acquire
commercial traits. Among the most decisive determinants influencing the
course of subsequent political evolution are whether or not a landed aristocracy has turned to commercial agriculture and, if so, the form that this
commercialization has taken. [Moore 1966: 419]

As is often the case, we see Moore attempting self-consciously to
extract a general principle of variation from the differences among the
specific cases at hand. At this point, Moore has turned decisively to
variation-finding comparison.

All this schematizing makes Moore sound like a historical bull-
dozer, scooping up chunks of experience to deposit them in great bins.

It hides the passion, length, and uncertainty of the search. (I recall leaving graduate school with a fistful of draft chapters and thoughtfully commented bibliographies from Moore's monumental work in progress and then returning years later to discover new versions of chapters and bibliographies in circulation, Moore still arguing with students, colleagues, and himself about the significance of his cases, and the book still in progress.) A good look at the language of *Social Origins* dispels that illusion; a reader notices Moore still reasoning the problems out, worrying about inconsistencies and gaps, taking the reader into the midst of the inquiry. The prose does not display the polish of a completed model, but the irregularity of a sustained, earnest discussion of vital, open questions.

Dennis Smith suggests, in fact, that Moore's deep concern for the moral and political significance of alternative paths of development sometimes led him to ignore or minimize factors whose influence he recognized readily in other contexts. In particular, says Smith, Moore (1) held to his image of rational human choice within well-defined structural limits where he should have recognized the influence of accumulated ideology, especially such justifications of rule as the northern bourgeoisie brought to power with them at the end of America's Civil War; (2) minimized the importance of international involvements, such as Britain's colonial conquests, which would be hard to reconcile both with the model of choice within structural limits and with Moore's characterization of democratic politics. Smith would not for a moment, however, advise Moore to leave his moral and political concerns at home. On the contrary:

Moore's approach to social analysis persistently draws out the implications for each other of theory and practice, empirical investigation and normative assessment, description and prescription, fact and value. Much of Moore's later work is an attempt to reinstate theory as a rational discussion of moral objectives and to relate this discussion to a reasoned evaluation of possible forms of practice. [Smith 1983: 171]

Yes, that is the point. In their great comparative inquiries, Marx and Weber repeatedly displayed their moral indignation, their concern that people should be oppressed, their zeal to discover the alternative paths to human liberation. Those passions did not keep them from wielding comparison with skill and imagination. Barrington Moore's *Social Origins of Dictatorship and Democracy* joins that great tradition.

8

ENCOMPASSING COMPARISONS

Encompassing the World

Encompassing comparisons begin with a large structure or process. They select locations within the structure or process and explain similarities or differences among those locations as consequences of their relationships to the whole. In everyday life, people use encompassing comparisons all the time: explaining the difference between two children's behavior by their orders of birth, attributing the characteristics of communities to their varying connections with a nearby metropolis, accounting for the behavior of executives in terms of their positions in the firm's organization chart. As self-conscious social science, nevertheless, encompassing comparison is rarer than individualizing, universalizing, or generalizing comparison.

Encompassing comparison demands a lot of its practitioners: Even to begin, they must have both a mental map of the whole system and a theory of its operation. To be sure, neither the map nor the theory need be correct at the start; so long as the provisional placements of units within the system and the explanations of their characteristics are self-correcting, map and theory will improve in use. Encompassing comparison also contains a great danger: It leads effortlessly to functional explanations, in which a unit behaves in a certain way **because**

of the consequences of its behavior for the system as a whole. Functional explanations, in their turn, are notoriously difficult to verify or falsify and slip into tautology with great ease. Lovers of risk should try encompassing comparisons.

Eric Wolf loves risks. In his sweeping *Europe and the People without History*, he undertakes to survey the cultural history of the entire world since 1492. He surveys with an eye to (1) mapping the connections among apparently distinct peoples in far corners of the earth; (2) explaining the descriptions Europeans gave of the supposedly primitive people they encountered in the course of colonial and commercial expansion; and (3) correcting an ethnography that faithfully portrayed as pristine, primitive, and independent those much-connected people who had already undergone extensive transformation in the course of their interactions with Europeans. Wolf's first page opens the barrage:

The central assertion of this book is that the world of humankind constitutes a manifold, a totality of interconnected processes, and inquiries that disassemble this totality into bits and then fail to reassemble it falsify reality. Concepts like "nation," "society," and "culture" name bits and threaten to turn names into things. Only by understanding these names as bundles of relationships, and by placing them back into the field from which they were abstracted, can we hope to avoid misleading inferences and increase our share of understanding. [Wolf 1982: 3]

To follow through from this bold beginning, Wolf divides his analysis into three parts: a sketch of alternate modes of production in the world of 1400, an analytic narrative of the European search for wealth in the rest of the world, and a description of the world division of labor under capitalism.

The book's basic design follows decent conventions: conditions before, conditions after, and changes linking them. Clearly, much depends on the accuracy of the middle section, which treats Iberians in America, the fur trade, the slave trade, and the web of European trade and conquest in the Orient. Refreshingly, the accounts teem with detail, the reconstructions of connections and changes ring true, yet the argument as a whole continues to develop. The conclusion of Wolf's analysis of the slave trade conveys the book's tone:

While Africa had long formed an integral part of the political and economic system of the Old World, European expansion after 1400 drew the continent into a traffic of global scale. The demand for African slaves reshaped the political economy of the entire continent. It gave rise, in one common process, to new tributary states and specialized organizations of slave hunters, and it turned societies described by anthropologists as "acephalous, segmented, lineage-based" into the predilect target populations of slavers. These different configurations cannot, therefore, be understood as typologically separable states or "tribes" of people without history. They are, rather, the variable outcomes of a unitary historical process. Nor can one understand Europe without a grasp of the role Africa played in its development and expansion. Leading participants in that growth were not only the European merchants and beneficiaries of the slave trade but also its African organizers, agents, and victims. [Wolf 1982: 230–31]

Rarely has anyone stated the case for encompassing comparison so well.

Early in his book, Wolf underlines the difference between his approach and the approaches of André Gunder Frank and Immanuel Wallerstein. For Wolf, Frank, and Wallerstein alike, the central place in the whole analysis belongs to the expansion of capitalism. All three explain the differences in the fates of various parts of the world in terms of their variable relationships to the expansion of capitalism.

There the separation begins. First of all, Frank and Wallerstein incline to a very large definition of the capitalist sphere. They concentrate on capital accumulation via exchange for profit and tend to treat all parties to unequal exchange as part of the same capitalist world system. Thus for them the European creation of worldwide markets dominated by their principal centers of trade and capital marked the opening of our own system. That happened in the fifteenth and sixteenth centuries. Capitalism, then, is a mode of exchange; the principles of capitalist production follow from the requirements of capitalist exchange.

For Wolf, capitalism is rather a distinctive mode of production. Following Ernest Mandel, he insists on production for profit by means of wage-labor as its hallmark. For Wolf, the expanding trade of the fifteenth to seventeenth centuries, for all its successful pursuit of profit and capital accumulation, represents mercantilism; true capitalism only became the dominant mode in the eighteenth century. It never became the universal mode.

Wolf's choice of the mode-of-production side in the continuing debate over the places of production and exchange in world capitalism complements his insistence on the independent contribution of the "people without history" to the history of the capitalist system. He utterly rejects the lumping together of the people far from the capitalist core in a peripheral zone of weak states and primitive peoples, sucked one by one into an orbit of dependency.

To some extent, Wolf's differences from dependency theorists represent the path by which he came to the problem in the first place. Frank and Wallerstein began by observing the influence of the core at the periphery (Frank mainly in Latin America, Wallerstein mainly in Africa), but then moved to the core in order to understand its actions: "Although they utilized the findings of anthropologists and regional historians, for both the principal aim was to understand how the core subjugated the periphery, and not to study the reactions of the micro-populations habitually investigated by anthropologists" (Wolf 1982: 23). Wolf wants to give those people back their history and then to rewrite the history of the "core" in consonance with that restitution. No contradiction, but a genuine division of labor.

Not all of Wolf's reshaping of history succeeds. Perhaps inevitably, the incentives for which Europeans undertook the subordination of distant people, the benefits they gained from their efforts, and the sources of their initial advantage in the struggle remain unclear. England's shift from production of sheep to manufacture of woolens from the fourteenth century onward, for instance, figures in Wolf's account as a pivotal event for the emergence of industrial capitalism. But Wolf offers no substantial explanation of the critical change.

More important, Wolf's concern to establish the long involvement of ostensibly isolated peoples in worldwide networks of trade, communication, and mutual influence drives much of his narrative. Summarizing the expansion of Spain and Portugal into the Americas, he stresses the creation (not the survival) in the highlands of a largely separate Indian sector. For lowland littorals and islands, he describes the systems of forced labor and cash-crop exports that Iberians put in place, but concludes with this characteristic observation:

Thus, African slaves and their descendants became the dominant population along the Atlantic coast of Brazil, on the Caribbean isles and littoral, and along the coast of Colombia, Ecuador, and Peru. Here they wrought, on the plantations and in the redoubts of runaway slaves, their own modes of adaptation and rebellion, in a history that is just beginning to be explored. [Wolf 1982: 157]

As a result of this preoccupation with new creations, Wolf neglects to ask seriously how the **extent** of involvement of a people in the portions of those networks dominated by Europeans affected the character of their social organization. If the idea of a continuum of assimilation to European ways distorts the history of the so-called people without history, what idea **does** account for their variety? Here, Wolf fails to use his encompassing comparisons to full advantage.

Stein Rokkan Encompasses

The late Stein Rokkan took a different tack from Frank, Wallerstein, and Wolf, but he relied on encompassing comparison as well. Like Immanuel Wallerstein, he made a decisive move from generalizing comparison, in which the cases stood as logically independent instances of the same phenomenon, to the preparation of a complete map of a single interdependent system. At both phases of Rokkan's intellectual career, an enduring problem lay at the center of his effort: Given the facts that people throughout the world vary enormously in their interests and aspirations, and that the political possibilities before them always correspond imperfectly to their interests and aspirations, what determines the concrete political means and outcomes that different groups of people actually have available to them? Why is it, for example, that the Swiss ended up with a centrifugal federal system, while the Scandinavian countries built rather centralized polities? Why do political parties seem to be more effective vehicles for action on the grievances of ordinary citizens in England than in France? Under what conditions can people approach direct democracy? The concrete questions varied, but the fundamental themes remained the same.

In struggling with these enduring problems, Stein Rokkan never settled for a reductionist explanation: not the reduction of political means and outcomes to the simple expression of the population's interests; not the reduction to variations in political institutions such as voting laws and party systems; not the reduction to a vague but enveloping political culture. As time went on, he turned increasingly to complex historical explanations. Confronted with a set of variations in contemporary political means and outcomes, he would move back in time, looking for the crucial choices: rapid or gradual, explicit or implicit—that set presumably different paths of development. Thus the precocity or lateness of industrialization, the historical dominance of landed or capitalist classes, the region's response to the Protestant Reformation, and many other features of a region's past became possible determinants of its present politics.

The same creative tension that drove all Rokkan's work informed his investigation of historical choice-points. The list of cruxes fluctuated and grew longer. In most trials, Rokkan was attempting to account for variation within Europe. In some of his later analyses, Rokkan worked with this set of "variables":

1 relationship of the region to the seven major migrations of peoples that left their residues across the European map;
2 extent and centrality of the region's urban networks;
3 subjection of the region to major empires;
4 religious outcome of the Reformation, including the encouragement or discouragement of distinctive written vernaculars;
5 organization of agricultural production.

Each of these items, obviously, contains more than one simple variable. Still, the list as a whole conveys a strong series of messages: not to rely on timeless, abstract schemes such as the "crises of development" (penetration, integration, participation, identity, legitimacy, distribution) with which Rokkan had been working ten years earlier; to insist on the interaction of economic, political, religious, and demographic factors; to ground the major variables in history. The idea, then, is to explain the differences among contemporary political systems—and, in this case, especially the political systems of peripheral areas such as his native Norway or his adopted Wales—as cumulative consequences of their region's connections to the chief differentiating processes which had earlier transformed Europe as a whole. Only then, Rokkan suggested, might it be useful to abstract and generalize concerning such questions as the effects of ethnic heterogeneity on party systems. We catch Rokkan slipping into encompassing comparison on the pretext of searching for generalizations.

Such a delay of the final score often reveals an author's loss of interest in the game. In Rokkan's case, however, the hope for an ultimate set of generalizations never seems to have disappeared. As he reviewed one of his later summaries of the European experience, for example, Rokkan outlined a world-wide set of variations among the world's geocultural areas. The "master variables" he singled out were:

1 secular/religious differentiation;
2 linguistic unification/distinctness;
3 differentiation/independence of city networks;
4 concentration/dispersion of landholdings. [Rokkan 1975: 592–95]

Whether Rokkan saw the world in the image of Europe or Europe in the image of the world is no doubt an idle question. Either way, the correspondence between this list and his diagramming of European history conveys a clear sense that the exploration of Europe yields information concerning the structure of the world at large. Either way, the actual enterprise consists of placing all of Europe within a consistent conceptual space.

Rokkan's "Conceptual Maps of Europe"

Stein Rokkan was a great inventor of conceptual devices. One of his more intriguing inventions took the form of "conceptual maps" summarizing the principles of geopolitical differentiation within Europe at various points in time. North/South differentiation, for example, always represented some version of the influence of Mediterranean events and structures—most commonly, the heritage left by the Roman Empire. Rokkan built and modified his conceptual maps in the same dialectical style he applied to his other work: picking up clues from other people's efforts at simplification, stating bold hypotheses only to qualify them immediately, constantly altering the categories, dimensions, and placements within them.

The very creation of the conceptual maps, indeed, occurred as part of the Rokkanian dialectic. In a semi-autobiographical statement of 1976, Rokkan explained that he turned to the cartographic effort out of dissatisfaction with the sorts of models of cleavage structure and of democratization he had presented in his *Citizens, Elections, Parties* (1970). Especially, he said, the model of democratization; it was

> too atomizing; it treated each case in isolation, without taking account of its connections with its surroundings, of the geopolitical position of the area in question. I began to study the links *in space* among the different cases, and became convinced of the decisive importance of *interregional relationships*, both in the process of nation-building and in the further structuring of mass mobilization. [Rokkan 1976: 9; emphasis in text]

Rokkan's intuition fell right on target. The most disconcerting feature of his earlier models is their implicit analogy with the giant cross-tabulations beloved of survey researchers: Large samples of ostensibly independent "cases," each one self-contained, line up neatly in rows and columns representing the abstract dimensions of theoretical importance.

The conceptual maps, as we shall see, did not banish this misleading analogy. They did reduce its scope. They helped him escape from the pernicious assumption that each of the states existing at the end of the process—say, the states of Europe at the end of World War II—corresponded to a distinct "society" that had a long, continuous history. Instead, Rokkan was able to portray those states as organizations growing up amid populations linked by long-stranded social networks and varying continuously in cultures and modes of production. More so than any of Rokkan's previous models, they pointed toward a genuinely interactive, historical account of European statemaking.

As of 1979, Rokkan was working with the two conceptual maps appearing in Figures 1 and 2. Figure 1 shows us his summary of the geography of major European ethnic clusters before the High Middle Ages. For practical purposes, some such distribution served as the baseline for all of Rokkan's historical analyses; he made no effort to explain the Roman Empire's pattern of influence or the processes of division, amalgamation, and migration that spread distinctive cultural groups across the European map. Thus we begin with some Celts (Welsh, Cornish, and Breton) inside the limits of the northern Roman Empire, and others (Scots and Irish) outside its limits. The conceptual map places the raw materials of European statemaking and political differentiation in a crude spatial grid.

FIGURE 1.

Rokkan's Geoethnic Map of Europe Before the High Middle Ages

	Atlantic Periphery	Coastal Plains	Central Plains and Alpine Territory		Landward Marchlands
Beyond the Reach of the Roman Empire	Icelanders Faeroese West Norse Celts: Scotland Ireland	East Norse Danes	Swedes		Finns Balts Prussians Poles, Lithuanians Moravians, Czechs
Territory of the Northern Empire	Celts: Wales Cornwall Brittany	Angles, Saxons Frisians, Jutes West Franks Gallo-Romans Normans	Germanic Tribes: Burgundians Saxons Alemannians Rhaetians	East Franks Thuringians Bavarians	Hungarians Bavarian settlers Tirolians
Mediterranean Territories	Basques	Occitans Catalans Corsicans Castilians Portuguese	Lombards Italians Sardinians Sicilians		Slovenes Croats Serbs

The map selects and looks forward in time. Practically none of the Arctic-dwellers appear in it. Along the eastern frontier, we look in vain for Ruthenians, Ukrainians, Wallachians, Macedonians, Kors, Vots, Letts, Turks, Greeks. The scheme distinguishes Lombards from Italians, but does not separate Piedmontese, Venetians, or Neapolitans. On the whole, an ethnic group has a much greater chance to show up on Rokkan's map if at some time after 1300 someone built a state dominated by people of that cultural origin.

Let me be clear and fair. Rokkan never claimed that the scheme provided more than a crude simplification of a complex process spread over centuries. With that understanding, the scheme has its uses. As Rokkan summarized:

These territorial distributions provided the ethnic-linguistic infrastructures for the institutional developments of the High Middle Ages; the first steps towards the consolidation of centralized monarchies, the early leagues of cities, the first consociational structures. In the next round, the distribution of ethnic identities and affinities determined the character and the cost of linguistic standardization within each of these territorial structures: the development of

FIGURE 2.

Rokkan's Conceptual Map of Europe, Sixteenth to Eighteenth Centuries*

THE "STATE-ECONOMY" DIMENSION: WEST-EAST AXIS

Zone	Seaward Peripheries	Seaward Empire-Nations		City-State Europe			Landward Empire-Nations		Landward Buffers
Characteristics of: Territorial Centres	WEAK	STRONG	STRONG	WEAK	WEAK	WEAK	STRONG	STRONG	WEAK
City Network	WEAK	STRONG	STRONG	STRONG	STRONG	STRONG	WEAK	WEAK	WEAK
Relationship to City-State Europe	DISTANT	DISTANT	CLOSE	Integrated into Larger System	Consociational Formation	Fragmented until 19th Century	CLOSE	DISTANT	
THE "STATE-CULTURE" DIMENSION: NORTH-SOUTH AXIS									
Protestant State Church	ICELAND NORWAY SCOTLAND WALES	ENGLAND	DENMARK**			HANSE GERMANY		SWEDEN	FINLAND
Mixed Territories					NETHERLANDS SWITZERLAND	RHINELAND	PRUSSIA		BALTIC TERRITORIES BOHEMIA
National Catholic	IRELAND BRITTANY		FRANCE	"Lotharingia" BURGUNDY ARELATUM			BAVARIA		POLAND
Counter-Reformation			SPAIN PORTUGAL	CATALONIA	BELGIUM	ITALY	AUSTRIA		HUNGARY

*Adapted for this volume by the author.

**States recognized as sovereign, 1648–1789, shown in italics.

such central standards was accelerated by the invention of printing and the religious conflicts of the Reformation and put the peripheries under heavy pressures to accept the norms set by the territorial centres. [Rokkan 1979: 1–32]

Thus, in Rokkan's view, the prior distribution of ethnic groups determined one of the major variations in the costs of subsequent statemaking, and helped determine which of Europe's territories and groups would become politically peripheral.

Rokkan's second conceptual map (Figure 2 shows its 1979 variant) lays out the distribution of political entities in Europe from the sixteenth to eighteenth centuries. It therefore stops history after enormous reshaping of the ethnic "raw materials," at a point when national states had already become the dominant organizations within the European continent, but were still struggling mightily to increase their power within their own territories, within Europe, and in the world as a whole. In fact, the names attached to different locations in the map introduce uncertainty about the reference date and about the units Rokkan had in mind: As states, no "Belgium" existed before 1830, no "Italy" before 1860. By that time, however, any political unit one might reasonably call "Burgundy" had long since crumbled into morsels gobbled up by France, Prussia, and the successors of the Habsburg empires. And so on through the map.

Clearly, the conceptual map has little value as an index to a precise historical moment or as a catalog of specific political units. Instead, it calls attention to systematic differences in the political experiences of people dwelling in various regions of Europe, as a function of their relationships to two major "axes" of development. Rokkan called the East-West line his "state-economy" axis. On the West, states that extracted surplus from a highly monetized economy, long stimulated by its involvement in seaborne trade. In the center, a band of tightly linked trading cities extending from northern Italy up to Flanders, surrounded by areas of intensive agriculture: city-state Europe. On the East, states that ultimately extracted their surplus from coerced agricultural labor. This axis, declared Rokkan,

reflects the fundamental asymmetry of the geopolitical structure of Europe: the dominant city network of the politically fragmented trade belt from the Mediterranean to the North, the strength of the cities in the territories con-

solidated to the seaward side of this belt, the weakness of the cities in the
territories brought together under the strong military centres on the landward
Marchland. [Rokkan 1979: 42]

The statemaking implications of the "state-economy" axis are evident.

The South-North dimension, in contrast, receives the name of
"state-culture" axis. There, according to Rokkan, we see the long-run
impact of the Roman Empire, as transmuted into the relative influence of the Roman Catholic church and its Orthodox sister in
parallel north-south strips of Europe. To the North, we find a band
in which national Protestant churches early marked off religious and
linguistic areas within which the barriers to the state's cultural penetration were relatively low. As we approach the South, we encounter
increasing degrees of religious "supraterritoriality," with corre-
spondingly higher barriers to cultural integration. In the Mediterranean band, according to the map's implicit argument, the strong presence of an international religious structure presented statemakers with
a serious rival, and ethnic particularists with a strong base for resistance
to national integration.

Despite the vagueness in its references to historical times, places,
peoples, and political units, Rokkan's conceptual map identifies some
principles of variation within Europe that other treatments of European political development regularly miss. If, following Rokkan's own
method, we add another band of Islamic territory—with that "su-
praterritorial" religious structure even more of a barrier to any
statemaker's capture of his subject population's exclusive allegiance
than in the old Roman Empire's heartland—to the south of Mediterranean Europe, and skew the "seaward" column eastward in that band
to represent the commercial significance of the Mediterranean, we get
a remarkably coherent sense of the major regional variations of state
structure.

To be sure, some predecessor made each of the major arguments
that Rokkan translated into an "axis," "dimension," or "band" of his
diagram; he worked largely by transmogrifying and assimilating other
people's monocausal structures. But the notion of an encompassing,
two-dimensional process of differentiation in Europe's human geography that limited the possibilities for statemaking in different corners of
the continent—that notion, so far as I know, was Rokkan's own invention.

The conceptual maps have some of the characteristic weaknesses of all Rokkan's major models. In a perceptive exegesis of Rokkan's political geography, Bertrand Badie remarks:

All in all, the variables Rokkan constructs in the course of his analysis are so numerous and defined so independently of one another that the conceptual map that results provides no more than an orderly juxtaposition of individual cases, each one representing an irreducible form of state- and nation-building. As compared with the methods of [Perry] Anderson and [Immanuel] Wallerstein, this method has the advantage of offering a more detailed and complex summary of the differences among European societies. On the other hand, it abandons any effort at an integrated, hierarchical explanation of political development, and thus moves away from sociological analysis, and the universal phenomena that analysis seeks to illuminate. Beyond the debate on the autonomy of politics, we begin to witness the confrontation between two different approaches, two different ways to use history in a developmental perspective. Anderson and Wallerstein turn to an historical method in order to show how differentiation occurs as a result of the operation of a factor they have previously defined as fundamental to national development; in contrast, Rokkan uses history to make an empirical review, by means of "retrospective diachronic analysis," of all the factors that might somehow have influenced the various observable forms of change; but he cannot gauge their weights or their interrelations. [Badie 1980: 115–16]

Badie's judgment is a bit harsh. Like a seasoned tabulator of survey responses, Rokkan implicitly invoked two interpretive principles: a rule of variance-reduction and a rule of parsimony. He preferred variables that reduced the unexplained variance. For a given amount of variance-reduction, he preferred a smaller **number** of variables.

Conscientiously followed, the two principles sometimes lead an investigator to spurious and/or superficial explanations. But they also urge the investigator to eliminate distinctions that do not make a difference, to give priority to distinctions that make a difference in a wide range of cases, and to undertake motivated choices among variables that overlap extensively. If we were to indict Rokkan's applications of the principles of variance-reduction and parsimony, it would surely be for excessive zeal: for seeking to eradicate *all* the unexplained variation, and for incessantly inserting new variables in the search for the Great Underlying Variable.

At a minimum, Rokkan's procedure has the merit of clarifying what we have to explain. A significant part of the literature purporting to deal with "political development," after all, consists of sketches of explanations for things that never happened: standard sequences of political institutionalization, the achievement of national integration, and so on. A good deal of the same literature, furthermore, misconstrues the European experience: imagining it, for example, to consist of a series of approximations, more or less successful, to British parliamentary democracy. In these intellectual circumstances, we must welcome an empirically grounded specification of what the analysts of European political change actually have to explain.

The geographical distribution identified by Rokkan cries out for explanation: why the central band of commercial cities and their hinterlands long and successfully resisted integration into large national states, why culturally homogeneous and autonomous states concentrated disproportionately along the northwestern frontier, and on down the inventory. In addition, Rokkan's axes themselves pose significant explanatory problems: If the initial sway of the Catholic church over everyday social relations does not explain the marked South/North differences in the creation of national churches strongly controlled by their respective states, what does? Isn't it true, as Rokkan suggests, that their immediate access to commercial cities made it easier for the statemakers of Europe's western regions to bypass great landlords and raise essential revenues from trade? Stein Rokkan's conceptual maps make such questions clearer and more pressing.

At that point, however, Bertrand Badie's complaint begins to gain force. The number of "variables" that visibly affected the direction taken by one European state or another is very large. Even with the wide variety of political units Rokkan takes into consideration, no strictly empirical sorting of the multiple European experiences can come close to identifying the crucial variables, eliminating the incidental variables, or specifying the relations among the variables. By itself, Rokkan's search procedure leads to an endless alternation of thesis and antithesis, without synthesis.

More important, the conceptual maps ultimately fail to accomplish the objective for which they originally seemed well suited: the examination of spatially ordered links among political histories. Having clearly started an encompassing comparison, Rokkan repeatedly veered back toward the language and practice of variation-finding comparison. Despite some intriguing hints of interdependence, the scheme as a whole presents the various national experiences as individual "cases" displaying the results of being subjected to different combinations of "variables." But Sweden, to take an obvious instance, is not simply a "case" located somewhere in the northern reaches of a giant cross-tabulation. The Sweden that appears on Rokkan's conceptual map is a shrunken remainder of the expansive power that at one time or another dominated Norway, Finland, Estonia, Livonia, and other important parts of the North. Can we reconstruct the political development of Sweden—or, for that matter, of Norway, Finland, Estonia, and Livonia—without taking that interaction directly into account? As a Norwegian, Stein Rokkan was acutely aware of Sweden's long hegemony in the North. Yet his scheme tends to reduce the known facts of international power to effects of similar positions within an abstract grid.

In the last analysis, Rokkan's schemes have a remarkable flatness. They press all the past into the same plane: conditioning variables for the present. As historical schemes, they lack the essential historical ingredient: time. The previous histories of Sweden, Norway, Denmark, and Finland are not merely accumulated residues; they are crooked paths. The early steps on those paths limit the later ones, and the paths taken by neighbors influence each other. The conceptual maps lack dynamism.

What's Wrong? What Should We Do About It?

Faced with that critique, I suppose Stein Rokkan would have smiled, run his fingers through his bushy hair, and replied, "Yes, that's right. How do you think we should get those international connections in?" He was the first to discount the current version of his model, to bemoan the connections it missed, to look for ways of altering it to deal more adequately with historical realities. With such a man, one did not hesitate to criticize. But, the criticism stated and discussed, one always felt a certain desire to help. Rokkan's influence endures: the work left unfinished in 1979 invites us to take up the task and continue the search for better formulations.

On the questions addressed by his conceptual maps, where did Stein

Rokkan leave the task? Let us recognize the value of those maps. First, they help us see that there **was** a spatial order to the development of national states in Europe—an order that such classifications as center/semi-periphery/periphery simply do not capture. Second, they make a case for the independent importance of variations in religious organization (or of other factors strongly correlated with religious organization) as an influence on the builders of states in different parts of Europe. Third, they identify unequivocally the danger in building schemes of political development retrospectively, starting with France, Great Britain, Italy, Spain, and the other twenty-odd states that now divide up the European continent, and acting as if the explanatory problem were to fit a causal model to the internal transformations of just those states.

Finally, Stein Rokkan's conceptual maps cast new light on an old paradox: the fact that capitalism and national states grew up together, and presumably depended on each other in some way, yet capitalists and centers of capital accumulation often offered concerted resistance to the extension of state power. Rokkan's emphasis on the network of trading cities brings out the probabilities that (1) where those networks were dense, local capitalists had an interest in resisting incorporation into strong states, and the means of defending that interest; (2) access to the taxable trade organized by those cities, and to the capital accumulated within them, gave crucial advantages to statemakers whose territories lay athwart, or adjacent to, the dense trading networks; (3) only late, gradually, and incompletely did the masters of European states nationalize the capital on which they drew, both in the sense of ensuring that capital accumulating within a state's effective territory was at the disposition of that state and no others, and in the sense of relying mainly on local capital for the credit and financial administration required to meet the state's operating expenses; and (4) the statemakers of eastern Europe, unlike their counterparts to the west, had compelling reasons for relying heavily on their region's landlords, and for clamping both the peasantry and the urban classes under tight controls.

More generally, Rokkan's conceptual maps embody an important hypothesis. We might outline it this way:

1   In a broad sense, statemakers and would-be statemakers in all parts of Europe were aiming at similar ends, but

2 both the means to accomplish those ends and the strategic problems posed by threats and opportunities in adjacent areas varied systematically by location within the continent, and

3 the different approaches to statemaking taken as a consequence of those variations in means and strategic problems produced significantly different political structures, region by region.

The hypothesis is important precisely because it is not self-evident. To the extent that we consider the structure of a state to result directly from the interests of its dominant classes, for example, we will doubt that statemakers in different parts of Europe were, indeed, pursuing similar ends and will be more inclined to attribute systematic geopolitical variation to the geography of dominant classes and their interests. Rokkan's scheme recognizes the significance of that geography of interests, but treats it as a set of constraints on aspiring statemakers rather than as the prime determinant of their interests.

In this light, the greatest flaw of the argument embedded in the conceptual maps is one I have not mentioned at all. The argument does not say why the people who built different kinds of states undertook the effort in the first place. Were they simply attempting to build up their personal power by whatever means were available? Did they have a vision, however dim and faulty, of the sort of structure they were struggling to create? Did states take shape as unintended byproducts of efforts directed to other ends? I do not know whether Stein Rokkan ever addressed these questions directly, or what reply he would have given them in 1979. I regret not having asked him.

For my own part, I think the answer is : some of each. The people who extended the power of national states were surely attempting, on the whole, to advance the interests of their own families, of their own factions, of the classes to which they belonged. The vision they had occasionally showed the influence of a doctrine or an historical memory, but most often represented the condition of a rival: The point was to create an organization sufficiently effective to check, or even vanquish, that rival. Yet the state structures that actually took shape grew largely as unintended by-products of other activities.

Which activities? The question helps us to become more specific about the elements missing from Rokkan's scheme. The interactions of war-making, taxation, and capital accumulation profoundly shaped European statemaking. Europeans did not undertake those three great activities with the intention of creating centralized, differentiated, autonomous, far-reaching political organizations—national states. Nor did they ordinarily foresee that organizations of that sort would emerge as a consequence of the pursuit of war-making, taxation, and capital accumulation.

To put it very, very crudely: The people who controlled European states (and organizations that eventually became the cores of states) made war in order to hold off, or to master, their competitors, and thus to enjoy the fruits of power within a secure, or even expanding, territory. The large number of similarly situated competitors promoted the adoption of new military technologies that conferred even a slight competitive advantage on their users. But new technologies generally cost more than those they replaced.

To make more effective war, powerholders therefore attempted to locate more capital. In the short run, they might acquire that capital by conquest, by selling off their assets, by coercing or dispossessing accumulators of capital. In the long run, the quest involved them in establishing regular access to capitalists who could supply and arrange credit and in imposing one form of regular taxation or another on the people and activities within their own territories. As the process went on, they developed a durable interest in promoting the accumulation of capital, sometimes in the guise of direct return to their own enterprises, sometimes in order to assure the availability of capital to borrow and tax, sometimes to forward the interests of the capitalists on whom they relied for financing.

All these activities generated organization: the creation of standing armies, the establishment of services to supply those armies, the institution of tax-collecting bureaucracies, the shaping of banks, markets, and mints. Statemakers did not seek to create the organization; they sought to sustain the activity. Among successful statemakers, the more difficult the extraction of the essential resources the bulkier the organization the activity brought into being. The organization statemakers created to sustain military activity and its complements hardened into the apparatus of a national state: durable, centralized, differentiated, autonomous, powerful.

My account is willfully crude and incomplete. It ignores the variation between the experiences of a highly centralized France and a federated Netherlands. It neglects the effects of different approaches to collecting taxes. It may well be wrong. I certainly have provided no evidence here for its correctness.

To the extent that it is plausible, nevertheless, this line of argument indicates what **kind** of effort would most effectively continue Stein Rokkan's inquiry: his underlying search for the origins of the political means and outcomes available to different groups of Europeans. A further tracing of the geographic variations identified by Rokkan's conceptual maps will not yield large intellectual returns; the maps have served their purpose. In general, the next round of work must examine the interactions among contenders for power and their consequences for the creation of new political structures. In particular, the interactions involved in war-making, taxation, and the accumulation of capital deserve the closest attention.

9

CONCLUSIONS

The Tasks at Hand

In the light of any formal logic of comparison, most of the inquiries we have been examining are ungainly indeed. On the scale of continents, national states, and regions, the matching of instances with each other only provides the grossest of natural experiments. Therein lie two traps: the trap of refinement and the trap of despair.

It is tempting to look for finer and finer comparisons, with larger numbers of cases and more variables controlled. In the present state of our knowledge of big structures and large processes, that would be a serious error. It would be an error because with the multiplication of cases and the standardization of categories for comparison the theoretical return declines more rapidly than the empirical return rises. Only in building better theories by means of comparisons on the scale of a Bendix, a Skocpol, a Moore or a Rokkan will we manage to shift that curve of theoretical return from finer comparison. In a distant future, we can aim to have theories of large-scale social processes sufficiently precise that a well-measured chunk of a single region's experience will provide strong proof of a theory's validity or invalidity.

The trap of despair opens up when we decide that such a day will never come—**can** never come. If we can never get past hesitant generalizations in the style of Stein Rokkan, what's the use?

The use is this: Historically grounded huge comparisons of big structures and large processes help establish what must be explained, attach the possible explanations to their context in time and space, and sometimes actually improve our understanding of those structures and processes. Rokkan's conceptual maps of Europe, for all their faults, do not simply differ from models of state-by-state political development. They have more explanatory power. They are better models.

In the improvement of our understanding, individualizing comparisons, universalizing comparisons, variation-finding comparisons, and encompassing comparisons all have their uses. In fact, they are somewhat different uses. I have described the four as if they were alternative tools for the same task. That helpful simplification will eventually have to give way. The four types of comparison differ, after all, with respect to the sorts of statements they yield rather than with respect to the logic of comparison as such. Their relative value depends on the intellectual task at hand. It also depends on the nature of the social world and the limits to our knowledge of that world. Pragmatic, ontological, and epistemological realities all matter.

Pragmatically, there are times when what we need most is a clear understanding of the singularities of a particular historical experience. If people have done a good deal of theorizing, implicitly or explicitly, on the basis of that experience, getting those singularities right will serve immediate theoretical purposes. The English experience in creating parliamentary government and regularized opposition needs scrutiny over and over again because—as the contrasting accounts of Bendix and Moore suggest—that experience appears, transmuted and generalized, in so much argument about the bases of democracy. In that case, individualizing comparison serves quite a general end.

Universalizing comparison, if appropriate and well done, has rare clarifying power. To show that the same sequence or conjunction of cause and effect recurs in widely separated settings reduces the intellectual need to erect separate explanatory frameworks for each setting, sharpens our sensitivity to other similarities and differences among settings, and helps identify forms of intervention in those settings that are likely to affect them. Suppose that demographers' long search for a standard sequence of transition, population by population, from high, unstable to low, stable mortality and fertility finally pays off. Knowledge of the sequence will cast intense light on the probable demo-

graphic consequences of various programs of investment, employment, agrarian reform, or fertility control.

Variation-finding comparison, however, promises to help us make
sense of social structures and processes that never recur in the same
form, yet express common principles of causality. None of the analyses
reviewed in this book, for example, provides much assurance that
anyone will ever discover a single path leading diverse regions from
low income to high income. Yet it remains possible that some correlates of change in income (for example, the tendency of populations to
spend smaller shares of their income on food and shelter as income
rises) will prove to be quite general. Variation-finding comparison will
identify and confirm those regularities.

Encompassing comparison, nevertheless, will often lead to alternative explanations of structures and processes that seem to yield to
variation-finding. If the essential determinant of a structure or process
is the connection of the social unit in which it appears to a whole
system of social relationships, the connection frequently produces effects which seem to be autonomous properties of the social unit itself.
Thus the use of the coup d'etat as the standard form of succession to
state power surely depends, at least in part, on the power and autonomy of the armed forces relative to that of any other organizations
within the same state.

Suspicion of some such regularity has led many analysts to search
for roots of military power and autonomy in poverty, underdevelopment, or tribal ideology. But the explanation of military power and
autonomy could lie mainly outside the states in question; armed forces
could well gain relative power and autonomy within their own spheres
to the extent that great powers provided arms, equipment, training,
and military advisers to their states, and the amount of that military
support could well depend on the geopolitical relationships of the
states in question to the world's great powers. In that case, an encompassing comparison would lead to a better explanation.

Yet the relative value of the four types of comparison in social
analysis ultimately depends on ontology and epistemology: the actual
structure of the social world and the limits of our ability to apprehend
that structure. If the structures and processes to which we give grand
names actually consist of unique creations having their own internal
logics and nothing in common but the names, or if we have no way of

discerning their common properties, then universalizing, variation-finding, and encompassing comparisons will yield spurious results: at best, observations of regularities in our perceptions.

If the world does, indeed, divide into coherent, autonomous societies whose operations are fully accessible to human understanding, then universalizing and variation-finding comparisons will lead to the truth, while individualizing and encompassing comparisons will serve at best as auxiliaries. If, however, social life really takes shape as a series of networks, vast or small but rarely well-bounded, which humans can identify and comprehend reliably, then all four varieties of comparison will have their places in inquiry, and encompassing comparison will come into its own. I am betting on this last possibility.

If you join me in the bet, you will probably agree that individualizing, universalizing, and variation-finding comparisons all have secure places in our intellectual toolbox. As scholars continue to use the various forms of comparison, my main hopes are that they will move increasingly to the historically grounded comparison of limited numbers of experiences and that on the way they will cast off whatever remains of the pernicious nineteenth-century postulates concerning big structures and large processes.

Encompassing comparisons, however, deserve more attention than they have received. Encompassing comparisons have twin advantages: directly taking account of the interconnectedness of ostensibly separate experiences and providing a strong incentive to ground analyses explicitly in the historical contexts of the structures and processes they include.

If we move up from the macrohistorical plane in which this book has worked to world-systemic and world-historical analyses, the importance of encompassing comparison increases, as the feasibility of universalizing and variation-finding comparison declines. For our own time, it is hard to imagine the construction of any valid analysis of long-term structural change that does not connect particular alterations, directly or indirectly, to the two interdependent master processes of the era: the creation of a system of national states and the formation of a worldwide capitalist system. We face the challenge of integrating big structures, large processes, and huge comparisons into history.

BIBLIOGRAPHY

NOTE: This bibliography includes every item cited in the book, as well as a selection of titles illustrating the problems and approaches discussed in the book. I have canted the selection toward books and toward works in English.

A. V. Ado
1971   *Krest'ianskoie dvizhenie vo frantsii vo vremiia velikoi burjhuaznoi revoliutsii kontsa XVIII veka*. Moscow: Izdatel'stvo Moskovskovo Universiteta.

Risto Alapuro
1976   "Regional Variation in Political Mobilization: On the Incorporation of the Agrarian Population into the State of Finland, 1907–1932." *Scandinavian Journal of History* 1: 215–42.

Gabriel A. Almond, Scott C. Flanagan and Robert J. Mundt, eds.
1973   *Crisis, Choice, and Change: Historical Studies of Political Development*. Boston: Little, Brown.

Gabriel A. Almond and G. Bingham Powell
1966   *Comparative Politics: A Developmental Approach*. Boston: Little, Brown.

Perry Anderson
1974   *Lineages of the Absolutist State*. London: NLB.

Michael Armer and Allen D. Grimshaw, eds.
1973   *Comparative Social Research: Methodological Problems and Strategies*. New York: Wiley.

Raymond Aron
1965   *Main Currents in Sociological Thought*. Vol. 1: *Montesquieu, Comte, Marx, Tocqueville* and *The Sociologists and the Revolution of 1848*. New York: Basic Books.

Robert Axelrod
1984   *The Evolution of Cooperation*. New York: Basic Books.

—— and William D. Hamilton
1981   "The Evolution of Cooperation." *Science* 211: 1390–96.

Bertrand Badie
1980   *Le développement politique*. 2nd ed. Paris: Economica.

1983   *Culture et politique*. Paris: Economica.

—— and Pierre Birnbaum
1979   *Sociologie de l'Etat*. Paris: Bernard Grasset.

Paul Bairoch
1970   *Diagnostic de l'évolution économique du Tiers-Monde 1900–1968*. 4th ed. Paris: Gauthier-Villars.

1976a   *Commerce extérieur et développement économique de l'Europe au XIXe siècle*. Paris: Mouton and Ecole des Hautes Etudes en Sciences Sociales.

1976b   "Europe's Gross National Product, 1800–1975." *Journal of European Economic History* 5: 273–340.

1977   *Taille des villes, conditions de vie et développement économique*. Paris: Editions de l'Ecole des Hautes Etudes en Sciences Sociales.

1982   "International Industrialization Levels from 1750 to 1980." *Journal of European Economic History* 11: 269–334.

—— and Maurice Lévy-Leboyer, eds.
1981   *Disparities in Economic Development since the Industrial Revolution*. London: Macmillan.

Arthur S. Banks and Phillip M. Gregg
1971   "Grouping Political Systems: Q-Factor Analysis of A Cross-Polity Survey." In *Macro-Quantitative Analysis*, edited by John V. Gillespie and Betty A. Nesvold. Beverly Hills, Calif.: Sage.

Samuel Barnes
1979   *Political Action: Mass Participation in Five Western Democracies*. Beverly Hills, Calif.: Sage.

Reinhard Bendix
1956   *Work and Authority in Industry: Ideologies of Management in the Course of Industrialization*. New York: Wiley.

1960   *Max Weber: An Intellectual Portrait*. Garden City, N.Y.: Doubleday.

1963   "Concepts and Generalizations in Comparative Sociological Studies." *American Sociological Review* 28: 532–39.

1977   *Nation-Building and Citizenship: Studies of Our Changing Social Order*. New enlarged edition; first published in 1964. Berkeley: University of California Press.

1978   *Kings or People: Power and the Mandate to Rule*. Berkeley: University of California Press.

Maxine Berg
1980   *The Machinery Question and the Making of Political Economy, 1815–1848*. Cambridge: Cambridge University Press.

——, Pat Hudson and Michael Sonenscher, eds.
1983   *Manufacture in Town and Country Before the Factory*. Cambridge: Cambridge University Press.

Albert Bergesen
    1980   "Official Violence during the Watts, Newark, and Detroit Race Riots of the
            1960s." In A Political Analysis of Deviance, edited by Pat Lauderdale. Min-
            neapolis: University of Minnesota Press.

Philippe Besnard, ed.
    1983   The Sociological Domain: The Durkheimians and the Founding of French Sociol-
            ogy. Cambridge: Cambridge University Press.

Geoffrey Best
    1982   War and Society in Revolutionary Europe, 1770–1870. London: Fontana.

Jerome Blum
    1978   The End of the Old Order in Rural Europe. Princeton; N.J.: Princeton University
            Press.

Friedhelm Boll
    1981   Massenbewegungen in Niedersachsen 1906–1920. Bonn: Verlag Neue Gesell-
            schaft.

Kenneth A. Bollen
    1979   "Political Democracy and the Timing of Development." American Sociological
            Review 44: 572–87.

Victoria Bonnell
    1980   "The Uses of Theory, Concepts and Comparison in Historical Sociology." Com-
            parative Studies in Society and History 22: 156–73.

    1983   Roots of Rebellion: Workers' Politics and Organizations in St. Petersburg and
            Moscow, 1900–1914. Berkeley: University of California Press.

Tom Bottomore and Robert Nisbet, eds.
    1978   A History of Sociological Analysis. New York: Basic Books.

Larry S. Bourne and James Simmons
    1983   "The Canadian Urban System." In Urbanization and Settlement Systems, by L.
            S. Bourne et al. Oxford: Oxford University Press.

Fernand Braudel
    1979   Civilisation matérielle, économie, et capitalisme, XVe–XVIIIe siècle. 3 vols. Paris:
            Armand Colin.

Rudolf Braun
    1977   "Steuern und Staatsfinanzierung als Modernisierungsfaktoren: Ein Deutsch-
            Englischer Vergleich." In Studien zum Beginn der modernen Welt, edited by
            Reinhard Koselleck. Stuttgart: Klett-Cotta.

Robert Brenner
    1976   "Agrarian Class Structure and Economic Development in Pre-Industrial
            Europe." Past and Present 70: 30–74.

    1977   "The Origins of Capitalist Development: A Critique of Neo-Smithian Marxism."
            New Left Review 104: 25–92.

Crane Brinton
    1965   The Anatomy of Revolution. Revised and expanded edition; first published in
            1938. New York: Vintage.

Richard Maxwell Brown and Don E. Fehrenbacher, eds.
    1977   Tradition, Conflict, and Modernization: Perspectives on the American Revolution.
            New York: Academic Press.

William Brustein
1983 "French Political Regionalism, 1849–1978." In *The Microfoundations of Macrosociology*, edited by Michael Hechter. Philadelphia: Temple University Press.

Michael Burawoy
1982 "Introduction: The Resurgence of Marxism in American Sociology." *American Journal of Sociology* 88 Supplement: S1–S30.

John C. Caldwell
1981 "The Mechanisms of Demographic Change in Historical Perspective." *Population Studies* 35: 5–27.

David Cannadine
1980 "Urban Development in England and Canada in the Nineteenth Century: Some Comparisons and Contrasts." *Economic History Review*, 2nd series, 33: 309–25.

Marina Cattaruzza
1979 *La formazione del proletariato urbano: Immigrati, operai di mestiere, donne a Trieste dalla metà del secolo XIX alla prima guerra mondiale.* Turin: Musolini.

Gian Primo Cella, ed.
1979 *Il movimento degli scioperi nel XX secolo.* Bologna: Il Mulino.

Andrew Charlesworth
1982 "A Comparative Study of the Spread of the Agricultural Disturbances of 1816, 1822 and 1830." Working Paper no. 9, Liverpool Papers in Human Geography, Department of Geography, University of Liverpool.

————, ed.
1983 *An Atlas of Rural Protest in Britain, 1548–1900.* London: Croom Helm.

Christopher Chase-Dunn
1979 "Comparative Research on World-System Characteristics." *International Studies Quarterly* 23: 601–23.

Serge Chassagne
1981 "Aspects des phénomènes d'industrialisation et de désindustrialisation dans les campagnes françaises au XIXe siècle." *Revue du Nord* 63: 35–58.

Louis Chevalier
1958 *Classes laborieuses et classes dangéreuses.* Paris: Plon.

Ronald H. Chilcote and Dale L. Johnson, eds.
1983 *Theories of Development: Mode of Production or Dependency?* Beverly Hills, Calif.: Sage.

Daniel Chirot
1977 *Social Change in the Twentieth Century.* New York: Harcourt Brace Jovanovich.

Nazli Choucri and Robert C. North
1975 *Nations in Conflict: National Growth and International Violence.* San Francisco: Freeman.

Lillian J. Christman, William R. Kelly and Omer R. Galle
1981 "Comparative Perspectives on Industrial Conflict." *Research in Social Movements, Conflict and Change* 4: 67–93.

Jerome Clubb and Erwin K. Scheuch, eds.
1980 *Historical Social Research: The Use of Historical and Process-Produced Data.* Stuttgart: Klett-Cotta.

Bernard S. Cohn
   1980   "History and Anthropology: The State of Play." *Comparative Studies in Society and History* 22: 198–221.

Randall Collins
   1980   [Review of Theda Skocpol, *States and Social Revolutions*]. *Theory and Society* 9: 647–51.

Auguste Comte
   1963   *Discours sur l'esprit positif.* First published in 1844. Paris: Union Générale d'Editions. "10/18".

Werner Couze and Ulrich Engelhardt, eds.
   1979   *Arbeiter im Industrialisierungsprozess: Herkunft, Lage und Verhalten.* Stuttgart: Klett-Cotta.

Frederick Cooper
   1981   "Africa and the World Economy." *African Studies Review* 24: 1–86.
   1983   "Urban Space, Industrial Time, and Wage Labor in Africa." In *Struggle for the City: Migrant Labor, Capital, and the State in Urban Africa,* edited by Frederick Cooper. Beverly Hills, Calif.: Sage.

Lewis A. Coser
   1979   "The Sources of Revolt" [Review of Theda Skocpol, *States and Social Revolutions*], *New York Times Book Review,* October 21, 1979, pp. 44–45.

Martha Crenshaw, ed.
   1983   *Terrorism, Legitimacy, and Power: The Consequences of Political Violence.* Middletown, Conn.: Wesleyan University Press.

Phillips Cutright, Michael Hout and David R. Johnson
   1976   "Structural Determinants of Fertility in Latin America: 1800–1970." *American Sociological Review* 41: 511–27.

James Chowning Davies
   1979   "The J-Curve of Rising and Declining Satisfactions as a Cause of Revolution and Rebellion." In *Violence in America: Historical and Comparative Perspectives;* edited by Hugh Davis Graham and Ted Robert Gurr. Beverly Hills, Calif.: Sage.

———, ed.
   1971   *When Men Revolt and Why.* New York: Free Press.

Jacques Delacroix and Charles Ragin
   1978   "Modernizing Institutions, Mobilization, and Third World Development: A Cross-National Study." *American Journal of Sociology* 84: 123–50.

Mattei Dogan and Dominique Pelassy
   1983   *How to Compare Nations: Strategies in Comparative Politics.* Chatham, N.J.: Chatham House.

W. T. Easterbrook
   1957   "Long Period Comparative Study: Some Historical Cases." *Journal of Economic History* 17: 571–95.

J. Medina Echavarria and Philip M. Hauser
   1961   "Rapporteur's Report." In *Urbanization in Latin America,* edited by Philip M. Hauser. New York: International Documents Service.

Harry Eckstein
   1980   "Theoretical Approaches to Explaining Collective Political Violence." In *Handbook of Political Conflict,* edited by Ted Robert Gurr. New York: Free Press.

S. N. Eisenstadt
   1963   *The Political Systems of Empires: The Rise and Fall of the Historical Bureaucratic Societies.* Glencoe, Ill.: Free Press.
   1966   *Modernization, Protest and Change.* Englewood Cliffs, N.J.: Prentice-Hall.
   1978   *Revolution and the Transformation of Societies: A Comparative Study of Civilizations.* New York: Free Press.
   1982   "Vergleichende Analyse der Staatenbildung in historischen Kontexten." In *Entstehung und Strukturwandel des Staates,* edited by Stefan Breuer and Hubert Treiber. Opladen: Westdeutscher Verlag.

Jon Elster
   1977   "Ulysses and the Sirens: A Theory of Imperfect Rationality." *Social Science Information* 16: 469–526.
   1982   "Marxism, Functionalism, and Game Theory: The Case for Methodological Individualism." *Theory and Society* 11: 453–82. Replies by G. A. Cohen, Philippe van Parijs, John E. Roemer, Johannes Berger, Claus Offe, Anthony Giddens, pp. 483–540.

Samuel E. Finer
   1982   "The Morphology of Military Regimes." In *Soldiers, Peasants, and Bureaucrats: Civil-Military Relations in Communist and Modernizing Regimes,* edited by Roman Kolkowicz and Andrzej Korbonski. London: Routledge & Kegan Paul.

Michael Fores
   1981   "The Myth of a British Industrial Revolution." *History* 66: 181–98.

John Foster
   1974   *Class Struggle and the Industrial Revolution: Early Industrial Capitalism in Three English Towns.* London: Weidenfeld & Nicolson.

André Gunder Frank
   1978   *World Accumulation, 1492–1789.* New York: Monthly Review Press.
   1979   *Dependent Accumulation and Underdevelopment.* New York: Monthly Review Press.
   1983   "Crisis and Transformation of Dependency in the World-System." In *Theories of Development: Mode of Production or Dependency?,* edited by Ronald H. Chilcote and Dale L. Johnson. Beverly Hills: Sage.

George M. Fredrickson
   1980   "Comparative History." In *The Past Before Us: Contemporary Historical Writing in the United States,* edited by Michael Kammen. Ithaca, N.Y.: Cornell University Press.

Rainer Fremdling and Richard Tilly, eds.
   1979   *Industrialisierung und Raum: Studien zur regionale Differenzierung im Deutschland des 19. Jahrhunderts.* Stuttgart: Klett-Cotta.

Dov Friedlander
   1983   "Demographic Responses and Socioeconomic Structure: Population Processes in England and Wales in the Nineteenth Century." *Demography* 20: 249–72.

Samuel Friedman
   1983   "Game Theory and Labor Conflict: Limits of Rational Choice Models." *Sociological Perspectives* 26: 375–97.

Harriet Friedmann
   1978   "World Market, State, and Family Farm: Social Bases of Household Production in the Era of Wage Labor." *Comparative Studies in Society and History* 20: 545–86.

William A. Gamson, Bruce Fireman and Steve Rytina
    1982   *Encounters with Unjust Authority.* Homewood, Ill.: Dorsey.

David Gaunt
    1977   "Pre-Industrial Economy and Population Structure: The Elements of Variance in
            Early Modern Sweden." *Scandinavian Journal of History* 2: 183–210.

Florence Gauthier
    1977   *La voie paysanne dans la Révolution française: L'Exemple picard.* Paris: Maspéro.

Ernest Gellner
    1983   *Nations and Nationalism.* Ithaca, N.Y.: Cornell University Press.

Gino Germani
    1971   "General Report [on Latin America]." In Institut International des Civilisations
            Différentes, *Les agglomérations urbaines dans les Pays du Tiers Monde: Leur rôle
            politique, social et économique.* Brussels: Editions de l'Institut de Sociologie, Uni-
            versité Libre de Bruxelles.

Alexander Gerschenkron
    1962   *Economic Backwardness in Historical Perspective.* Cambridge, Mass.: Harvard
            University Press.

John V. Gillespie and Betty A. Nesvold, eds.
    1971   *Macro-Quantitative Analysis: Conflict, Development and Democratization.* Bev-
            erly Hills, Calif.: Sage.

Robert Glen
    1984   *Urban Workers in the Early Industrial Revolution.* London: Croom Helm.

Jack A. Goldstone
    1982   "The Comparative and Historical Study of Revolutions." *Annual Review of
            Sociology* 8: 187–207.

J. D. Gould
    1979   "European Inter-Continental Emigration 1815–1914: Patterns and Changes."
            Journal of European Economic History 8: 593–680.

Christian Gras and Georges Livet, eds.
    1977   *Régions et régionalisme en France du XVIIIe siècle à nos jours.* Paris: Presses
            Universitaires de France.

Raymond Grew
    1980   "The Case for Comparing Histories." *American Historical Review* 85: 763–78.
——, ed.
    1978   *Crises of Political Development in Europe and the United States.* Princeton, N.J.:
            Princeton University Press.

R. D. Grillo
    1980   *"Nation" and "State" in Europe: Anthropological Perspectives.* New York: Aca-
            demic Press.

Ted Robert Gurr
    1969   *Why Men Rebel.* Princeton, N.J.: Princeton University Press.
——, Peter N. Grabosky and Richard C. Hula
    1977   *The Politics of Crime and Conflict: A Comparative History of Four Cities.* Beverly
            Hills, Calif.: Sage.

Robert L. Hamblin, R. Brooke Jacobsen and Jerry L. L. Miller
    1973   *A Mathematical Theory of Social Change.* New York: Wiley.

Theodore S. Hamerow
  1958   *Restoration, Revolution, Reaction: Economics and Politics in Germany, 1815–1871.* Princeton, N.J.: Princeton University Press.

E. A. Hammel
  1980   "The Comparative Method in Anthropological Perspective." *Comparative Studies in Society and History* 22: 145–55.

Michael Hanagan
  1980   *The Logic of Solidarity: Artisans and Industrial Workers in Three French Towns, 1871–1914.* Urbana: University of Illinois Press.

Russell Hardin
  1982   *Collective Action.* Baltimore: Johns Hopkins University Press for Resources for the Future.

Lawrence E. Hazelrigg and Maurice A. Garnier
  1976   "Occupational Mobility in Industrial Societies: A Comparative Analysis of Differential Access to Occupational Ranks in Seventeen Countries." *American Sociological Review* 41: 498–510.

Michael Hechter
  1975   *Internal Colonialism: The Celtic Fringe in British National Development, 1536–1966.* Berkeley: University of California Press.
  1977   "Lineages of the Capitalist State." *American Journal of Sociology* 82: 1057–74.
——, ed.
  1983   *The Microfoundations of Macrosociology.* Philadelphia: Temple University Press.
—— and William Brustein
  1980   "Regional Modes of Production and Patterns of State Formation in Western Europe." *American Journal of Sociology* 85: 1061–94.

Hugh Heclo
  1974   *Modern Social Politics in Britain and Sweden: From Relief to Income Maintenance.* New Haven: Yale University Press.

Louis Henry and Didier Blanchet
  1983   "La Population de l'Angleterre de 1541 à 1871." *Population* 38: 781–821.

David Herlihy
  1981   "Numerical and Formal Analysis in European History." *Journal of Interdisciplinary History* 12: 115–36.

Elbaki Hermassi
  1978   "Changing Patterns in Research on the Third World." *Annual Review of Sociology* 4: 239–57.

Philippe-J. Hesse
  1979   "Géographie coutumière et révoltes paysannes en 1789." *Annales Historiques de la Révolution Française* 51: 280–306.

J. H. Hexter
  1983   "The Birth of Modern Freedom." *Times Literary Supplement,* January 21, 1983, pp. 51–54.

Douglas A. Hibbs
  1973   *Mass Political Violence: A Cross-National Causal Analysis.* New York: Wiley.
  1978   "On the Political Economy of Long-Run Trends in Strike Activity." *British Journal of Political Science* 8: 153–75.

Christopher Hill
  1972   *The World Turned Upside Down: Radical Ideas during the English Revolution.*
          New York: Viking.

Jerome L. Himmelstein and Michael S. Kimmel
  1981   "States and Revolutions: The Implications and Limits of Skocpol's Structural
          Model." *American Journal of Sociology* 86: 1145–54.

Ernst Hinrichs, Eberhard Schmitt and Rudolf Vierhaus, eds.
  1978   *Vom Ancien Regime zur französischen Revolution: Forschungen und Perspektiven.*
          Göttingen: Vandenhoeck & Ruprecht.

Albert O. Hirschman
  1977   *The Passions and the Interests: Political Arguments for Capitalism Before Its
          Triumph.* Princeton, N.J.: Princeton University Press.

John Hobcraft and Philip Rees
  1977   *Regional Demographic Development.* London: Croom Helm.

Steve Hochstadt
  1982   "Social History and Politics: A Materialist View." *Social History* 7: 75–83.

Dirk Hoerder
  1977   *Crowd Action in Revolutionary Massachusetts, 1765–1780.* New York: Academic
          Press.

Robert T. Holt and John E. Turner
  1966   *The Political Basis of Economic Development: An Exploration in Comparative
          Political Analysis.* Princeton, N.J.: Van Nostrand.

————, eds.
  1970   *The Methodology of Comparative Research.* New York: Free Press.

Terence K. Hopkins, et al.
  1982   *World-Systems Analysis: Theory and Methodology. Explorations in the World-
          Economy,* vol. 1. Beverly Hills, Calif.: Sage.

Lynn Avery Hunt
  1978   *Revolution and Urban Politics in Provincial France: Troyes and Reims 1786–
          1790.* Stanford, Calif.: Stanford University Press.

  1984   *Politics, Culture, and Class in the French Revolution.* Berkeley: University of
          California Press.

Ronald Inglehart
  1977   *The Silent Revolution: Changing Values and Political Styles Among Western
          Publics.* Princeton, N.J.: Princeton University Press.

Alex Inkeles
  1975   "The Emerging Social Structure of the World." *World Politics* 27: 467–95.

  1976   "Understanding and Misunderstanding Individual Modernity." In *The Uses of
          Controversy in Sociology,* edited by Lewis A. Coser and Otto N. Larsen. New
          York: Free Press.

  1981   "Convergence and Divergence in Industrial Societies." In *Directions of Change:
          Modernization Theory, Research, and Realities,* edited by Mustafa O. Attir et al.
          Boulder, Colo.: Westview Press.

———— and David Smith
  1974   *Becoming Modern: Individual Change in Six Developing Countries.* Cambridge,
          Mass.: Harvard University Press.

James H. Jackson, Jr.
1979 "Wanderungen in Duisburg während der Industrialisierung 1850–1910." In *Moderne Stadtgeschichte*, edited by Wilhelm Heinz Schröder. Historisch-Sozial-wissenschaftliche Forschungen, 8. Stuttgart: Klett-Cotta.

Carl Jantke and Dietrich Hilger, eds.
1965 *Die Eigentumslosen: Der deutsche Pauperismus und die Emanzipationskrise in Darstellungen und Deutungen der zeitgenossischen Literatur.* Freiburg and Munich: Karl Alber.

Barbara Hockey Kaplan, ed.
1978 *Social Change in the Capitalist World Economy.* Beverly Hills, Calif.: Sage.

Nikki R. Keddie
1983 "The Iranian Revolution in Comparative Perspective." *American Historical Review* 88: 579–98.

Hermann Kellenbenz, ed.
1975 *Agrarisches Nebengewerbe und Formen der Reagrarisierung im Spätmittelalter und 19./20. Jahrhundert.* Stuttgart: Gustav Fischer.

William R. Kelly, Dudley L. Poston, Jr. and Phillips Cutright
1983 "Determinants of Fertility Levels and Change among Developed Countries: 1958–1978." *Social Science Research* 12: 87–108.

Harold R. Kerbo
1982 "Movements of 'Crisis' and Movements of 'Affluence': A Critique of Deprivation and Resource Mobilization Theories." *Journal of Conflict Resolution* 26: 645–63.

Clark Kerr
1960 "Changing Social Structures." In *Labor Commitment and Social Change in Developing Areas*, edited by Wilbert E. Moore and Arnold S. Feldman. New York: Social Science Research Council.

Michael Kidron and Ronald Segal
1981 *The State of the World Atlas.* New York: Simon & Schuster.

Michael Kidron and Dan Smith
1983 *The War Atlas: Armed Conflict–Armed Peace.* New York: Simon & Schuster.

Peter Kriedte, Hans Medick and Jürgen Schlumbohm
1977 *Industrialisierung vor der Industrialisierung: Gewerbliche Warenproduktion auf dem Land in der Formationsperiode des Kapitalismus.* Göttingen: Vandenhoeck and Ruprecht.

Stein Kuhnle
1973 *Social Mobilization and Political Participation: The Nordic Countries, c. 1850–1970.* Bergen: Institute of Sociology.

Witold Kula
1960 "Secteurs et régions arriérés de l'économie du capitalisme naissant." *Studi Storici* 1: 569–85.

Simon Kuznets
1960 *Modern Economic Growth: Rate, Structure, and Spread.* New Haven, Conn.: Yale University Press.

Bernard Lacroix
1981 *Durkheim et le* [sic] *politique.* Paris: Presses de la Fondation Nationale des Sciences Politiques.

Frederic C. Lane
    1958   "Economic Consequences of Organized Violence." *Journal of Economic History*
            18: 401–17.

R. Lawton
    1973   "Rural Depopulation in Nineteenth Century England." In *English Rural Com-
            munities: The Impact of a Specialised Economy*, edited by Dennis R. Mills.
            London: Macmillan.

Ronald Lee, ed.
    1977   *Population Patterns in the Past.* New York: Academic Press.

W. R. Lee, ed.
    1972   *European Demography and Economic Growth.* London: Croom Helm.

Georges Lefebvre
    1947   *The Coming of the French Revolution.* Princeton, N.J.: Princeton University
            Press.

    1959   *Les paysans du Nord pendant la Révolution française.* First published in 1924.
            Bari: Laterza.

Gerhard Lenski
    1966   *Power and Privilege.* New York: McGraw-Hill.

Pierre Léon, François Crouzet and Raymond Gascon, eds.
    1972   *L'Industrialisation en Europe au XIXe siècle: Cartographie et Typologie.* Paris:
            Editions du Centre National de la Recherche Scientifique.

Daniel Lerner
    1968   "Comparative Analysis of Processes of Modernization." In *Comparative Research
            across Cultures and Nations*, edited by Stein Rokkan. Publications of the Interna-
            tional Social Science Council, 8. Paris: Mouton.

Ron J. Lesthaeghe
    1977   *The Decline of Belgian Fertility, 1800–1970.* Princeton, N.J.: Princeton Univer-
            sity Press.

David Levine
    1977   *Family Formation in an Age of Nascent Capitalism.* New York: Academic Press.

Arend Lijphart
    1971   "Comparative Politics and the Comparative Method." *American Political Science
            Review* 65: 682–93.

Juan J. Linz and Amando de Miguel
    1966   "Within-Nation Differences and Comparisons: The Eight Spains." In *Comparing
            Nations: The Use of Quantitative Data in Cross-National Research*, edited by
            Richard L. Merritt and Stein Rokkan. New Haven, Conn.: Yale University Press.

Catarina Lis and Hugo Soly
    1979   *Poverty and Capitalism in Pre-Industrial Europe.* Atlantic Highlands, N.J.:
            Humanities Press.

Kenneth A. Lockridge
    1983   *The Fertility Transition in Sweden: A Preliminary Look at Smaller Geographic
            Units, 1855–1890.* Umeå: Demographic Data Base, Umeå University.

Alf Lüdtke
    1980   "Genesis und Durchsetzung des modernen Staates: Zur Analyse von Herrschaft
            und Verwaltung." *Archiv für Sozialgeschichte* 20: 470–91.

Ian Maitland
    1983   *The Causes of Industrial Disorder: A Comparison of a British and a German Factory.* London: Routledge & Kegan Paul.

Ted Margadant
    1979   *French Peasants in Revolt: The Insurrection of 1851.* Princeton, N.J.: Princeton University Press.

Peter V. Marsden and Nan Lin, eds.
    1982   *Social Structure and Network Analysis.* Beverly Hills, Calif.: Sage.

Robert M. Marsh
    1967   *Comparative Sociology: A Codification of Cross-Societal Analysis.* New York: Harcourt, Brace & World.

Sture Martinius
    1977   *Peasant Destinies: The History of 552 Swedes Born 1810–12.* Stockholm: Almqvist & Wiksell.

Peter Mathias and Patrick O'Brien
    1976   "Taxation in Britain and France 1715–1810: A Comparison of the Social and Economic Incidence of Taxes Collected for the Central Governments." *Journal of European Economic History* 5: 601–50.

Peter D. McClelland
    1975   *Causal Explanation and Model Building in History, Economics, and the New Economic History.* Ithaca, N.Y.: Cornell University Press.

William H. McNeill
    1982   *The Pursuit of Power: Technology, Armed Force and Society since A.D. 1000.* Chicago: University of Chicago Press.

Hans Medick
    1976   "The Proto-Industrial Family Economy: The Structural Function of Household and Family During the Transition from Peasant Society to Industrial Capitalism." *Social History* 3: 291–315.

Franklin L. Mendels
    1978   "Aux origines de la proto-industrialisation." *Bulletin du Centre d'Histoire Economique et Sociale de la Région Lyonnaise* no. 2 (1975): 1–25.

Louis-Sebastian Mercier
    1982   *Parallèle de Paris et de Londres.* Edited by Claude Bruneteau and Bernard Cottret. Paris: Didier Erudition.

John Merriman, ed.
    1979   *Consciousness and Class Experience in Nineteenth Century Europe.* New York: Holmes & Meier.

John Merrington
    1975   "Town and Country in the Transition to Capitalism." *New Left Review* 93: 71–92.

Richard L. Merritt and Stein Rokkan
    1966   *Comparing Nations: The Use of Quantitative Data in Cross-National Research.* New Haven, Conn.: Yale University Press.

John W. Meyer and Michael T. Hannan, eds.
    1979   *National Development and the World-System: Educational, Economic and Political Change, 1950–1970.* Chicago: University of Chicago Press.

James H. Mittelman
    1981   *Underdevelopment and the Transition to Socialism: Mozambique and Tanzania.*
            New York: Academic Press.

Ephraim H. Mizruchi
    1983   *Regulating Society: Marginality and Social Control in Historical Perspective.* New
            York: Free Press.

Leslie Page Moch
    1983   *Paths to the City: Regional Migration in Nineteenth-Century France.* Beverly
            Hills, Calif.: Sage.

George Modelski
    1978   "The Long Cycle of Global Politics and the Nation-State." *Comparative Studies
            in Society and History* 20: 214–35.

Wolfgang J. Mommsen
    1982   "Non-Legal Violence and Terrorism in Western Industrial Societies: An Histor-
            ical Analysis." In *Social Protest, Violence and Terror in Nineteenth- and Twen-
            tieth-Century Europe,* edited by Wolfgang J. Mommsen and Gerhard Hirschfeld.
            New York: St. Martin's Press for the German Historical Institute, London.

Barrington Moore, Jr.
    1966   *Social Origins of Dictatorship and Democracy.* Boston: Beacon Press.
    1969   "Revolution In America?" *New York Review of Books,* January 30, 1969, pp.
            6–12.
    1978   *Injustice: The Social Bases of Obedience and Revolt.* White Plains, N.Y.: Sharpe.

Michel Morineau
    1981   "Un grand dessein: 'Civilisation matérielle, économie et capitalisme (XVe–
            XVIIIe Siècle); de Fernand Braudel." *Revue d'Histoire Moderne et Contemporaine*
            28: 623–68.

Richard L. Morrill
    1970   *The Spatial Organization of Society.* Belmont, Calif.: Duxbury Press.

Gary B. Nash
    1979   *The Urban Crucible: Social Change, Political Consciousness, and the Origins of
            the American Revolution.* Cambridge, Mass.: Harvard University Press.

Joan Nelson
    1979   *Access to Power: Politics and the Urban Poor in Developing Nations.* Princeton,
            N.J.: Princeton University Press.

Claude Nicolet
    1982   *L'Idée républicaine en France (1789–1924): Essai d'histoire critique.* Paris: Gal-
            limard.

Robert A. Nisbet
    1969   *Social Change and History: Aspects of the Western Theory of Development.* Lon-
            don: Oxford University Press.

Douglass C. North
    1983   "A Theory of Institutional Change and the Economic History of the Western
            World." In *The Microfoundations of Macrosociology,* edited by Michael Hechter.
            Philadelphia: Temple University Press.

Anthony Oberschall
    1978   "Theories of Social Conflict." *Annual Review of Sociology* 4: 291–315.

Patrick O'Brien
    1982   "European Economic Development: The Contribution of the Periphery." *Economic History Review*, 2nd series, 35: 1–18.

—— and Caglar Keyder
    1978   *Economic Growth in Britain and France 1780–1914: Two Paths to the Twentieth Century.* London: George Allen & Unwin.

Guillermo O'Donnell
    1980   "Comparative Historical Formations of the State Apparatus and Socio-Economic Change in the Third World." *International Social Science Journal* 32: 717–29.

Mancur Olson
    1982   *The Rise and Decline of Nations: Economic Growth, Stagflation, and Social Rigidities.* New Haven, Conn.: Yale University Press.

A. F. K. Organski and Jacek Kugler
    1980   *The War Ledger.* Chicago: University of Chicago Press.

Jeffery Paige
    1975   *Agrarian Revolution: Social Movements and Export Agriculture in the Underdeveloped World.* New York: Free Press.

Karen Ericksen Paige and Jeffery M. Paige
    1981   *The Politics of Reproductive Ritual.* Berkeley: University of California Press.

Talcott Parsons
    1937   *The Structure of Social Action.* New York: McGraw-Hill.

    1966   *Societies: Evolutionary and Comparative Perspectives.* Englewood Cliffs, N.J.: Prentice-Hall.

    1971a   "Comparative Studies and Evolutionary Change." In *Comparative Methods in Sociology: Essays on Trends and Applications,* edited by Ivan Vallier. Berkeley: University of California Press.

    1971b   *The System of Modern Societies.* Englewood Cliffs, N.J.: Prentice-Hall.

John Patten
    1973   Rural-Urban Migration in Pre-Industrial England. Research Papers, no. 6. Oxford: School of Geography.

Janice E. Perlman
    1976   *The Myth of Marginality: Urban Poverty and Politics in Rio de Janeiro.* Berkeley: University of California Press.

Elizabeth Perry
    1981   *Rebels and Revolutionaries in North China, 1848–1948.* Stanford, Calif.: Stanford University Press.

John C. Pierce and Richard A. Pride, eds.
    1972   *Cross-National Micro-Analysis: Procedures and Problems.* Beverly Hills, Calif.: Sage.

Abel Poitrineau
    1983   *Remues d'hommes: Les migrations montagnardes en France, 17e–18e siècles.* Paris: Aubier Montaigne.

Sidney Pollard
    1973   "Industrialization and the European Economy." *Economic History Review* 26: 636–48.

————, ed.
1980   *Region und Industrialisierung: Studien zur Rolle der Region in der Wirtschaftsges-chichte den letzten zwei Jahrhunderte.* Göttingen: Vandenhoeck & Ruprecht.

Donatella della Porta and Gianfranco Pasquino, eds.
1983   *Terrorismo e violenza politica: Tre casi a confronto: Stati Uniti, Germania e Giappone.* Bologna: Il Mulino.

Alejandro Portes and John Walton
1981   *Labor, Class, and the International System.* New York: Academic Press.

Pierre-Joseph Proudhon
1924   *De la Capacité politique des Classes ouvrières. Ouevres complètes de P.-J. Proudhon,* vol. 3. First published in 1865. Paris: Marcel Rivière.

Charles Ragin and David Zaret
1983   "Theory and Method in Comparative Research: Two Strategies." *Social Forces* 61: 731–54.

Mostafa Rajai
1977   *The Comparative Study of Revolutionary Strategy.* New York: McKay.

Melvin Richter
1977   *The Political Theory of Montesquieu.* Cambridge: Cambridge University Press.

Stein Rokkan
1970   *Citizens, Elections, Parties: Approaches to the Comparative Study of the Process of Development.* Oslo: Universitetsforlaget.

1975   "Dimensions of State Formation and Nation-Building: A Possible Paradigm for Research on Variations within Europe." In *The Formation of National States in Western Europe,* edited by Charles Tilly. Princeton, N.J.: Princeton University Press.

1976   "Une famille de modèles pour l'histoire comparée de l'Europe occidentale." Un-published paper presented to the Association Francaise de Science Politique.

1979   "Peripheries and Centres: The Territorial Structure of Western Europe." Unpublished draft of chapter 1, *Economy, Territory, Identity: The Politics of the European Peripheries.*

————, ed.
1968   *Comparative Research Across Cultures and Nations.* Paris: Mouton.

———— and Derek W. Urwin
1982   "Centres and Peripheries in Western Europe." In *The Politics of Territorial Identity: Studies in European Regionalism,* edited by Stein Rokkan and Derek W. Urwin. Beverly Hills, Calif.: Sage.

Gilbert Rozman
1976   *Urban Networks in Russia, 1750–1800, and Premodern Periodization.* Princeton, N.J.: Princeton University Press.

Richard Rubinson
1978   "Political Transformation in Germany and the United States." In *Social Change in the Capitalist World Economy,* edited by B. H. Kaplan. Beverly Hills, Calif.: Sage.

George Rudé
1959   *The Crowd in the French Revolution.* Oxford: Oxford University Press.

D. E. H. Russell
1974   *Rebellion, Revolution and Armed Force: A Comparative Study of Fifteen Countries with Special Emphasis on Cuba and South Africa.* New York: Academic Press.

Charles F. Sabel
1982   *Work and Politics: The Division of Labor in Industry.* Cambridge: Cambridge University Press.

Helen Icken Safa
1982   "Introduction." In *Towards a Political Economy of Urbanization in Third World Countries*, edited by Helen Icken Safa. Delhi: Oxford University Press.

Thomas C. Schelling
1967   "Economics and Criminal Enterprise," *Public Interest* 7: 61–78.

Erwin K. Scheuch
1966   "Cross-National Comparisons Using Aggregate Data: Some Substantive and Methodological Problems." In *Comparing Nations: The Use of Quantitative Data in Cross-National Research*, edited by Richard L. Merritt and Stein Rokkan. New Haven, Conn.: Yale University Press.

Wally Seccombe
1983   "Marxism and Demography." *New Left Review* 137: 22–47.

Edward Shorter
1969   "Middle Class Anxiety in the German Revolution of 1848." *Journal of Social History* 2: 189–215.

1973   "'La vie intime': Beiträge zu seiner Geschichte am Beispiel des kulturellen Wandels in den bayerischen Unterschichten im 19. Jahrhundert." *Kölner Zeitschrift für Soziologie und Sozialpsychologie*, Sonderheft 16: 530–49.

J. David Singer
1980   "Accounting for International War: The State of the Discipline." *Annual Review of Sociology* 6: 349–67.

G. William Skinner
1977   "Cities and the Hierarchy of Local Systems." In *The City in Late Imperial China*, edited by G. William Skinner. Stanford, Calif.: Stanford University Press.

Theda Skocpol
1973   "A Critical Review of Barrington Moore's *Social Origins of Dictatorship and Democracy*." *Politics and Society* 4: 1–34.

1977   "*Wallerstein's World Capitalist System: A Theoretical and Historical Critique*," *American Journal of Sociology* 82: 1075–89.

1979   *States and Social Revolutions: A Comparative Analysis of France, Russia, and China.* Cambridge: Cambridge University Press.

1982   "What Makes Peasants Revolutionary?" In *Power and Protest in the Countryside: Studies of Rural Unrest in Asia, Europe, and Latin America*, edited by Robert P. Weller and Scott E. Guggenheim. Durham, N.C.: Duke University Press.

——— and Margaret Somers
1980   "The Uses of Comparative History in Macrosocial Inquiry." *Comparative Studies in Society and History* 22: 174–97.

——— and Ellen Kay Trimberger
1978   "Revolutions and the World-Historical Development of Capitalism." *Berkeley Journal of Sociology* 22: 101–13.

Melvin Small and David J. Singer
   1982   *Resort to Arms: International and Civil Wars, 1816–1980.* Beverly Hills, Calif.:
           Sage.

Carol A. Smith
   1976   "Analyzing Regional Social Systems." In *Regional Analysis*, edited by Carol A.
           Smith. Vol. 2 *Social Systems.* New York: Academic Press.

Dennis Smith
   1983   *Barrington Moore, Jr.: A Critical Appraisal.* Armonk, N.Y.: Sharpe.

Richard Smith
   1981   "Fertility, Economy and Household Formation in England over Three Cen-
           turies." *Population and Development Review* 7: 595–622.

David L. Snyder
   1975   "Institutional Setting and Industrial Conflict: Comparative Analyses of France,
           Italy and the United States." *American Sociological Review* 40: 259–78.

——— and Edward L. Kick
   1979   "Structural Position in the World-System and Economic Growth, 1955–1970: A
           Multiple Network Analysis of Transnational Interactions." *American Journal of
           Sociology* 84: 1096–1126.

Pitirim A. Sorokin
   1947   *Society, Culture and Personality.* New York: Harper & Row.

Evelyne Huber Stephens
   1980   *The Politics of Worker's Participation: The Peruvian Approach in Comparative
           Perspective.* New York: Academic Press.

Arthur L. Stinchcombe
   1965   "Social Structure and Organizations." In *Handbook of Organizations*, edited by
           James G. March. Chicago: Rand McNally.

   1967   [Review of Barrington Moore, Jr., *Social Origins of Dictatorship and Democracy*].
           Harvard Educational Review 37: 290–93.

   1968   *Constructing Social Theories.* New York: Harcourt Brace & World.

   1975   "Social Structure and Politics." In *Handbook of Political Science*, edited by Fred I.
           Greenstein & Nelson W. Polsby. Vol. 3: *Macropolitical Theory.* Reading, Mass.:
           Addison-Wesley.

   1976   "Marxist Theories of Power and Empirical Research." In *The Uses of Controversy
           in Sociology*, edited by Lewis A. Coser and Otto N. Larsen. New York: Free Press.

   1978   *Theoretical Methods in Social History.* New York: Academic Press.

   1983   *Economic Sociology.* New York: Academic Press.

Lawrence Stone
   1967   "News from Everywhere" [review of Barrington Moore, Jr., *Social Origins of
           Dictatorship and Democracy*]. *New York Review of Books*, August 24, 1967, pp.
           31–35.

Jan Sundin and Eric Soderlund, eds.
   1979   *Time, Space and Man: Essays in Microdemography.* Stockholm: Almqvist &
           Wiksell International.

Francis X. Sutton
   1982   "Rationality, Development, and Scholarship." *Social Science Research Council
           Items* 36: 49–57.

Alexander Szalai
    1972   *The Use of Time: Daily Activities of Urban and Suburban Populations in Twelve Countries.* The Hague and Paris: Mouton.

Sidney Tarrow
    n.d.
    [1983]   "Struggling to Reform: Social Movements and Policy Change During Cycles of Protest." Occasional Paper no. 15, Center for International Studies, Cornell University.

John G. Taylor
    1979   *From Modernization to Modes of Production: A Critique of the Sociologies of Development and Underdevelopment.* Atlantic Highlands, N.J.: Humanities Press.

Charles Tilly, Louise A. Tilly and Richard Tilly
    1975   *The Rebellious Century, 1830–1930.* Cambridge, Mass.: Harvard University Press.

Louise A. Tilly
    1982   "Three Faces of Capitalism: Women and Work in Nineteenth Century French Cities." In *French Cities in the Nineteenth Century,* edited by John Merriman. London: Hutchinson.

    1983   "People's History and Social Science History." *Social Science History* 7: 457–74.

Richard Tilly
    1980   *Kapital, Staat, und sozialer Protest in der deutschen Industrialisierung.* Göttingen: Vandenhoeck & Ruprecht.

Richard M. Titmuss
    1970   *The Gift Relationship: From Human Blood to Social Policy.* London: George Allen & Unwin.

Alexis de Tocqueville
    1978   *Souvenirs.* Written in 1850–51; first published in 1893. Paris: Gallimard.

Per Torsvik, ed.
    1981   *Mobilization, Center-Periphery Structures and Nation-Building.* A volume in commemoration of Stein Rokkan. Bergen: Universitetsforlaget.

Arnold J. Toynbee
    1947   *A Study of History.* One-volume abridgement of vols. 1–6 by D. C. Somervell. New York: Oxford University Press.

Clive Trebilcock
    1981   *The Industrialization of the Continental Powers, 1780–1914.* London: Longman.

C. N. Vakil
    1971   "General Report [on Asia]." In Institut International des Civilisations Différentes, *Les agglomérations urbaines dans les Pays du Tiers Monde: Leur rôle politique, social et économique.* Brussels: Editions de l'Institut de Sociologie, Université Libre de Bruxelles.

Ivan Vallier, ed.
    1971   *Comparative Methods in Sociology: Essays on Trends and Applications.* Berkeley: University of California Press.

Katherine Verdery
    1983   *Transylvanian Villagers: Three Centuries of Political, Economic and Ethnic Change.* Berkeley: University of California Press.

Jan deVries
    1978   "Barges and Capitalism: Passenger Transportation in the Dutch Economy, 1632–
                1839." A. A. G. *Bijdragen* 21:33–398.

Peter Wallensteen
    1973   *Structure and War: On International Relations 1920–1968*. Stockholm: Raben &
                Sjogren.

Immanuel Wallerstein
    1974,   *The Modern World System*. 2 vols. New York: Academic Press.
    1980

    1976   "Modernization: Requiescat in Pace." In *The Uses of Controversy in Sociology*,
                edited by Lewis A. Coser and Otto N. Larsen. New York: Free Press.

    1980   "Braudel le 'Annales,' e la Storiografia contemporanea." *Studi Storici* 21: 5–18.

John Walton
    1984   *Reluctant Rebels: Comparative Studies of Revolution and Underdevelopment*.
                New York: Columbia University Press.

Harvey Waterman
    1981   "Reasons and Reason: Collective Political Activity in Comparative and Historical
                Perspective." *World Politics* 23: 554–89.

Max Weber
    1972   *Wirtschaft und Gesellschaft*. 5th ed. Tubingen: J. C. B. Mohr.

Robert P. Weller and Scott E. Guggenheim, eds.
    1982   *Power and Protest in the Countryside: Studies of Rural Unrest in Asia, Europe,
                and Latin America*. Durham, N.C.: Duke University Press.

Harrison White
    1981   "Production Markets as Induced Role Structures." In *Sociological Methodology
                1981*. San Francisco: Jossey-Bass.

    n.d.   "Notes on the Constituents of Social Structure." Unpublished paper. Cambridge,
                Mass.: Harvard University

Gwyn W. Williams
    1968   *Artisans and Sans-Culottes: Popular Movements in France and Britain during the
                French Revolution*. London: Arnold.

Christer Winberg
    1975   *Folkökning och proletisering kring den sociala strukturomvandlingen på Sveriges
                Landsbygd under den agrara revolutionen*. Gothenburg: Historiska Institutionen i
                Goteborg.

Ian Winchester
    1972   "On Referring to Ordinary Historical Persons." In *Identifying People in the Past*,
                edited by E. A. Wrigley. London: Arnold.

Eric R. Wolf
    1982   *Europe and the People without History*. Berkeley: University of California Press.

Keith Wrightson
    1982   *English Society, 1580–1680*. London: Hutchinson.

——— and David Levine
    1979   *Poverty and Piety in an English Village: Terling, 1525–1700*. New York: Aca-
                demic Press.

E. A. Wrigley and R. S. Schofield
    1981   *The Population History of England 1541–1871.* Cambridge, Mass.: Harvard University Press.

Alfred Young, ed.
    1976   *The American Revolution: Explorations in the History of American Radicalism.* DeKalb: Northern Illinois University Press.

Perez Zagorin
    1982   *Rebels and Rulers, 1500–1660.* 2 vols. Cambridge: Cambridge University Press.

Morris Zelditch
    1971   "Intelligible Comparisons." In *Comparative Methods in Sociology: Essays on Trends and Applications,* edited by Ivan Vallier. Berkeley: University of California Press.

Ekkart Zimmerman
    1983   *Political Violence, Crises and Revolutions.* Cambridge, Mass.: Schenkman.

Aristide R. Zolberg
    1980   "Strategic Interactions and the Formation of Modern States: France and England." *International Social Science Journal* 32: 687–716.

ACKNOWLEDGMENTS

The author gratefully acknowledges permission to reprint material from the following:

From *Kings or People: Power and the Mandate to Rule* by Reinhard Bendix (University of California Press, 1978).

From *Social Origins of Dictatorship and Democracy* by Barrington Moore, Jr. Copyright © 1966 by Barrington Moore, Jr. Reprinted by permission of Beacon Press.

From *States and Social Revolution* by Theda Skocpol (Cambridge University Press, 1979).

From *Europe and the People without History* by Eric R. Wolf (University of California Press, 1982).

Stein Rokkan's "Geoethnic Map of Europe Before the High Middle Ages" (Figure 1, page 133) appeared previously in *The Formation of National States in Western Europe*, edited by Charles Tilly, copyright © 1975 by Princeton University Press, pages 578–579. It is reprinted here with the permission of Princeton University Press.

Rokkan's "Conceptual Map of Europe, Sixteenth to Eighteenth Centuries" (Figure 2, page 134) is an adaptation of the map that appeared in "Territories, Centres, and Peripheries," by Stein Rokkan, in *Centre and Periphery: Spacial Variation in Politics*, edited by Jean Gottman, copyright © 1980 by Sage Publications, Inc., page 170. It is used here by permission of Sage Publications.

All quotations from foreign-language sources were translated by the author.

INDEX